1983

RASKOLNIKOV AND OTHERS

RASKOLNIKOV AND OTHERS

Literary Images of Crime, Punishment, Redemption, and Atonement

Edward Sagarin

City College and City University of New York

With a Foreword by
Marvin E. Wolfgang

ST. MARTIN'S PRESS • NEW YORK

Library of Congress Catalog Card Number: 80–51056
Copyright © 1981 by St. Martin's Press, Inc.
All Rights Reserved.
Manufactured in the United States of America.
54321
fedcba
For information, write St. Martin's Press, Inc.,
175 Fifth Avenue, New York, N. Y. 10010

cover design: Myrna Sharp
typography: Carolyn Eggleston

ISBN: 0–312–66397–8

To
Mary Sagarin, omnivorous reader,
and
Annie Weinberg, devoted friend

Contents

Foreword

Raskolnikov and Others is to be admired for its creative blending of literature as art and criminology as science. Novelists are not scientists, and the novelist who writes about crime and criminality is not a criminologist. Yet there is an intellectual territory which literature and scientific writing share. To break down a phenomenon, a concept, or a personality into its parts and describe the interrelationships, whether one is writing a novel or a scientific study, is to provide analysis. To find larger meanings, widen the scope to embrace other events, offer rival hypotheses or speculations is to provide interpretation. Both science and literary art engage in both of these activities. To be sure, the language differs: in *belles lettres* the style of presentation is likely to be looser, more freely drawn. But the logic of analysis and the intuitive understanding of interpretation occupy the work of both the literary artist and the scientist.

Moreover, the creative processes in literature and science stem from similar sources of the mind. Scientists serendipitously stumble on or logically create working hypotheses, test them, and draw conclusions. Writers do the same as they create plots and develop characters. Inspiration and creative imagination are found among both.

To focus more specifically on the subject of this volume, it might be said that the more we know about the criminal—the more we understand him and appreciate his conscious and unconscious motives—the more we may excuse him. This assertion is as true for scientific as for literary analyses of criminal behavior. However, the antiheroes of criminological science are more likely to become heroes or respectable social or psychological victims in novels. In *Raskolnikov and Others*, Professor Sagarin, a distinguished author of works on deviance and crime, draws this comparison to our attention.

One of Robert Nisbet's claims about artists and scientists must surely apply to our present author. Nisbet said: "The problems, insights, ideas and forms which come to the artist and to the scientist seem to come as often from the unconscious as the conscious mind, from wide, eclectic, and unorganized reading, observing, or experiencing, from musing, browsing, and dreaming, from buried experiences, as from anything immediately and consciously in view."* In this volume, Professor Sagarin has demonstrated the artistry in his science. The result is a masterly investigation in which an outstanding criminologist uses his professional perspective to analyze and interpret deviants created in the minds of some of our greatest writers. This is a book that social scientists, literary specialists, and literate general readers alike will find illuminating and delightful.

MARVIN E. WOLFGANG

---

* Robert Nisbet, *Sociology as an Art Form* (New York: Oxford University Press, 1976), p. 19.

Preface

This book grew out of a conviction that the world of literature and the world of criminology look at the same social realities and grapple with similar problems about the human being and the human condition. Yet these two worlds are hardly on speaking terms with each other. As a criminologist, I became increasingly convinced that our entire discipline would be enriched by looking carefully at the great writers whose insights into the meaning and nature of guilt, responsibility, punishment, and expiation are probably unequalled.

Two problems confronted me. The first was to delineate not merely the similarities in interest but also the distinctions between the method, scope, reliability, and techniques of the literary artist on the one hand and the behavioral scientist on the other. Secondly, I found myself with such a vast literature to choose from that I was distressed by what I would have to leave out were I to give space and attention to the six characters who are of greatest interest to me because they illuminate a number of different though closely intertwined themes. These themes are hinted at in the subtitle of this book: the search for an understanding of the mind and motivation of the transgressor; the need for punishment that comes from within and without; the enduring faith of human beings that they can find redemption by expiation, atonement, confession, and catharsis; and finally the possibility of salvation through suffering when all of us assume responsibility, individually and collectively, for our own actions.

At the City College of New York I was able to give a course covering the subject matter and content of this book. Attended by students of literature and criminology and by others about to enter law school or other fields, the discussions were heated and enthusiastic, the arguments many. When my colleagues in criminology learned of what I had done, I was besieged by requests: What literature did you discuss? Is this a workable way of teaching criminology? Out of the interests of students and colleagues, then, these essays came to be written.

I am indebted to many people who read these essays in earlier form and made suggestions, some of which I have incorporated into my work, and since I have not indicated personal debts in the course of the book, let me express them here. Robert J. Kelly of Brooklyn College and David W. McKinney, Jr., of the University of Guelph were so critical and so helpful that they deserve many footnotes stating that an idea, even an entire paragraph or page, came from them. Donal E. J. MacNamara and Margaret MacNamara both read the earlier drafts and gave me many suggestions. My colleagues at City College who did the same included William McCord and Steven Goldberg. And of course I am grateful to my students, as well as to other colleagues from a 1979 meeting of the Western Society of Criminology at which I delivered a paper that embodied some of the ideas in the pages that follow. Before these people had read early drafts and again after they read later ones, the manuscript was carefully gone over by my wife, Gertrude Sagarin, and my sister, Mary Sagarin. They were both critical and helpful, a welcome combination.

Now they are all thanked and exonerated, and sole responsibility falls on the writer. That is fitting, for after all, that we are all accountable for our own actions is the major message of this book.

EDWARD SAGARIN

RASKOLNIKOV AND OTHERS

In Search of Criminology Through Fiction

Among the most significant sources to which one goes for answers to age-old questions about the human condition, about the meaning of being a human being, about the nature of humanity and of the societies and cultures in which we live, is the legacy of literature, in the form of drama, poetry, and novels. Poverty and wealth, bereavement following death, forces that bring people together and drive them apart in a family, the nature of love and of war—all are depicted in the two millennia of literary work that is our heritage. Where are fatalism, incest, remorse, and self-punishment more forcefully portrayed than in Sophocles? Who can enlighten us more on the meaning of love than a long list of writers from Ovid to Lawrence? Where is the social evil arising from feuds between families and clans, and even by extension between nations, portrayed in all its tragic implications with greater understanding than by Shakespeare in *Romeo and Juliet?*

In this body of literature crime, redemption, and themes closely related hold a central position. For literally thousands of years, at least back to the era when the Old Testament was probably evolving as an oral literature, sin and the reaction against it—the reactions of both God and society—have been described, analyzed, and studied. In the earliest scenes of the Bible there is transgression and banishment, followed soon thereafter by fratricide, committed by the son of Adam and Eve. Thus humanity was only in its second generation—at least in this symbolic rendering of the origin of our species—when the first recorded murder occurred, and to this day the stigma borne by the transgressor is referred to as the mark of Cain.

Sexual violations were abundant in the Old Testament: seduction, incest, homosexuality. Problems of crime held the attention of Greek dramatists, Roman poets, and the writers of the Renaissance. Shakespeare delineated conspirators plotting murder, their suspicions, their consciences, entering into the minds and thoughts of Hamlet and his mother and uncle, of Lucrece and her attacker, and others. It was not only crime that dramatists and storytellers were depicting here, it was often suffering and atonement, expiation and redemption.

These are some of the major literary images, and side by side with them there grew up a body of thought, philosophic and later social scientific, concerned with the same themes. It was a dramatist but it might well have been a philosopher who wrote, *Homo sum; humani nil a me alienum puto* (Publius Terentius Afer, generally known as Terence: *I am a man; I count nothing human as alien to me*). But just what could be called human—was it anything that a human being had ever done or had the capacity to do?—remained unanswered by Terence, although it was a problem pursued by both philosophers and the builders of literature. There were in fact two bodies of literature growing, each looking at the same phenomena but in different ways, and they were not as entirely separate as at one time they might have appeared to be. After all, Rousseau was a novelist, as was Voltaire, and philosophic works, even scientific ones, were often written in the form of poetry.

There was a bifurcation, however, and literature in the artistic sense separated from social philosophy and social and behavioral science. If at times the former appears to be the more insightful, it is not to say that the latter is unproductive or that its contribution to this body of thought is unneeded, but that there was a parallel or complementary rather than a redundant development.

Criminology as a separate field of study flowered in the eighteenth and nineteenth centuries. It had been preceded by philosophic and theological inquiries into the nature of sin and transgression, and by the growth of criminal law and the rich and informed studies of the philosophy of law and of punishment. The interest in social science as science, given its great impetus in France and England during the first half of the nineteenth century, spurred the development of criminology. Then Darwin published *The Origin of Species,* and the era of evolution, anthropology, and biology was reflected in the growth and refinement of criminological thought, particularly in Italy.

In its parallel development with poetry, novels, and dramas dealing with the same basic issues that held the attention of criminologists—the motivations of people who transgress the laws, the nature of the reactions against them, and the struggle of such people to redeem themselves—criminology appears to have learned less from the literary masters than they had to teach, and the reverse is also true. Two groups of thinkers, both looking at the same object, were going their separate ways. Here and there one finds an exception, a major figure who bridges the gap, not by being both novelist and scientist or philosopher but by interweaving the knowledge of the two fields in a manner beyond what had previously been accomplished. Perhaps no one comes to mind in this regard more quickly than Freud, who drew upon Sophocles, Shakespeare, Dostoevsky, and Goethe and who in turn so strongly influenced Lawrence, Kafka, Joyce, and perhaps one might say all of twentieth-century literature.

Despite the rich influence that literature had on psychoanalysis and that the latter had in turn on the former (as witness the road from Sophocles and Dostoevsky to Freud and then from Freud to Joyce and Lawrence), it can nonetheless be stated that the two roads toward an understanding of humanity were parallel but hardly visible to each other. Only indirectly and unsystematically, on rare occasions, did the rich treasures of one group illuminate and fertilize the work of the other.

In 1959, C. P. Snow noted that in Western societies there were two cultures, one consisting of scientists (he was referring to physicists and chemists and not social scientists) and the other of writers, and that the two were totally ignorant of each other's work:

> I felt I was moving among two groups—comparable in intelligence, identical in race, not grossly different in social origin, earning about the same incomes, who had almost ceased to communicate at all, who in intellectual, moral and psychological climate had so little in common that instead of going from Burlington House or South Kensington to Chelsea, one might have crossed an ocean.[1]

It was not merely that they were not communicating with one another; it was, Snow contended, that "the intellectual life of the whole of Western society is increasingly being split into two polar groups."[2] There were literary intellectuals at one pole, and at the other the physical scientists.

It is perhaps less true of social scientists, in that they stand as a bridge or an island between the two poles, deeply interested in and involved in the work of physicists and chemists and certainly not unaware of what writers, the literary intellectuals, are saying about the social world. But it is also true that the relevance of literary output for social science and of social science for literature is more immediate, more complex, more demanding than Snow's two poles allow. So that if we now begin to think of three cultures and not two, with social scientists occupying a midway position between the other two, we find that to the extent that these groups represent what Snow called different cultures, the consequences can be even more disastrous than he had thought.

Criminology is a part of this midway culture, and at this point it is probably true that criminologists have more to learn from the literary world than the reverse. To say that criminologists have largely ignored the body of belles lettres, with the psychoanalysts as significant exceptions, is not to deny that some attention has been given to the problems posed and the answers proposed in works of fiction. The distinguished criminologist Gilbert Geis, in an essay on Jeremy Bentham, writes that Bentham presumably "does not consider the possibility that an outlawed act might actually serve to increase human happiness, . . . [that] the dilemma so brilliantly portrayed by Dostoevsky in *Crime and Punishment* in which a murder is defined, with considerable justification, as a social good by its perpetrator [is] thus morally justifiable."[3] Geis draws attention here to an important issue, and he goes to a novelist, not a criminologist, for an elaboration and a portrayal of it. That the study of Dostoevsky is exceptionally fruitful for the criminologist can be seen from the manner in which Geis, or another reader, could take the statement on the definition of the crime by its perpetrator as morally justifiable, and carry it further, noting that it was only when Raskolnikov abandoned this vision of his own act that he was able to move toward rebirth.

Dostoevsky is mentioned almost in passing by America's renowned criminologist Marvin E. Wolfgang, in an essay on Cesare Lombroso, often considered the founder of scientific criminology: "By his supporters Lombroso has been referred to as a scientific Columbus who opened up a new field for exploration, and his insight into human nature has been compared to that of Shakespeare and Dostoevsky. Perhaps these encomia are exaggerations."[4] What Wolfgang is here suggesting is that Lombroso's disciples had such a high opinion of him that they compared his insights into human nature with those of Dostoevsky (let us leave Shakespeare aside), and since such eulogistic remarks are thought of as possible exaggerations, the logic of the statement is that Dostoevsky's insights at least equalled if they did not surpass those of our greatest criminologists.

But was Dostoevsky himself a criminologist? Or Conrad or Faulkner or the others who make up the sextet whose works are discussed in these essays? Or Kafka, Camus, Sartre, Tolstoi, each for one work or many, or Proust for his colossal study of sex deviance, a field so closely related, at least at the time he wrote, to the concept of crime? Without conceding that there is any justification for the two cultures, or the three, to fail to communicate with one another and to draw from others and hence enrich themselves, it is still worthwhile to note the distinction between the literary intellectuals and the social scientists, even when they examine the same phenomenon. If, as Wolfgang contends, and as my next essay describes, Dostoevsky had insights into human nature surpassed by few, and specifically into the mind of the criminal in committing the act, in punishing himself, and in searching for redemption, what distinguishes him from the social scientist?

The distinction between novelist and social scientist is a difference of métier and method. What is involved here may well be two entirely different ways of portraying the same human behavior, and with it, entirely different ways of looking at, understanding, and explaining it. Sociology is itself an art form, writes Robert Nisbet, in an essay in which he contends that sociologists have been portraitists very much like those who use canvas or put words on paper.[5] Both look at social types, and both at social milieux. At the same time that sociologists were examining urbanization and its concomitant poverty and slums, cities and their squalor were the subject of the novels of Balzac, Gissing, Dickens, Zola, and many others. Novelists were describing workers' lives in factories and at home, and what better portrait of workers can one find than in the writings of Marx and Engels? The two groups, the literary artists (and others traditionally termed artists) and the social artists were using different techniques in looking at the same objects, in conveying the same messages, and in reaching similar conclusions. In the eighteenth and nineteenth centuries the lines of similarity were even greater, for many novelists were not yet dependent upon metaphor, which is probably the hallmark distinguishing art from exposition, explication, and science.

Perhaps Nisbet is here a bit sanguine, his examples all too nicely chosen to fit into his theme. If one arbitrarily demands that a work of art must be contemplated as a thing of beauty, that it must, to qualify as art, be not only metaphor but also inspire a sense of esthetic appreciation, then only a few social scientists would qualify as artists (Nisbet would, it might be added, more than an overwhelming number of his colleagues). He even stops to take to task one eminent sociologist for his failure not as an artist but as a scientist—for the failure to have empirical evidence of a scientific nature from which he can draw the intuitive conclusion that he does. That is precisely the license permitted to the artist, never to the scientist; the novelist does not need proof, he can convince us by intuiting the truth. In that sense, sociology is not an art form and should not aspire to be one; what is needed is the communication that Snow found lacking, so that sociology and art can draw inspiration from each other.

Criminologists have indeed given the world portraits of criminals and, in addition, of the detectives and police, of families of prisoners, and of victims. While many of these are in the form of endless tables and statistical correlations, sometimes important even when boring but seldom punctuated by anything deserving to be called insightful, this has not always been the case. Some criminologists and other social scientists have made portraits that differ only slightly from what Daniel Defoe had sought to accomplish with *Moll Flanders*. That book, in fact, is not only in the criminological tradition, it may well be a forerunner of such later works as descriptions of criminals by Hutchins Hapgood, of a professional thief by Edwin Sutherland, of a safe-breaker by Bill Chambliss, or of a professional fence by Carl Klockars. There is something of a straight line, a common intellectual core and alliance, that goes from Defoe to Oscar Lewis, from *Moll Flanders* to *The Families of Sanchez*.[6]

With the exception of Lewis, the writers wrote what came to be known as "own story" criminology, a technique developed by the prominent sociology department at the University of Chicago earlier in this century. Researchers ventured forth into the real world of hoboes and denizens of the slums and described what they found, sometimes in their own words and on occasion in the words of the subjects living there (itself a small difference, as an examination of a third-person narrative like Dostoevsky's and a first-person tale, as told by Defoe in *Moll Flanders*, will illustrate). Yet there are several differences that separate Defoe's *Moll Flanders* from Sutherland's *Professional Thief*, and although at this point the techniques of criminologist and novelist almost converge, they do not quite become identical. Three distinctions seem apparent.

First, Defoe's work is offered as fiction, Sutherland's as edited autobiography (with some slight changes to protect informers and preserve anonymity). That Sutherland may have more fiction in the work than he allowed or believed would not negate a basic difference.

Second, Defoe presents the story with a minimum of commentary, while Sutherland makes a running commentary as a sociologist-criminologist throughout the work. In fact, Sutherland's notes and analytic remarks are at least as important (if not more so) as the autobiographical confession of the thief, Chic Conwell (note the name, for I will be calling attention to names chosen by Faulkner and others in these essays). It is true, also, that Defoe departs from storytelling in its pure form more than a modern novelist would do, because the art of refraining from explication was not yet fully developed when he wrote.

Third, Moll Flanders is offered to the reader as one person, with one set of experiences. Whereas Chic Conwell is *explicitly* presented not as one particular professional thief but as one who represents many, an entire genre, Moll is *implicitly* portrayed in a similar manner. This is so in the sense that all art is universalistic in its implications: it never says something about just one character, one situation, or one setting; it talks about the human and social condition.

What, then, distinguishes the criminologists, or all social scientists, from novelists and other artists? Above all, it is method. The criminologist has come to a conclusion about crime and related subjects through studies based on selected (preferably carefully and scientifically selected) samples rather than on one or several individuals (Freud and theories drawn from a single case notwithstanding). The samples are or aspire to be representative; just of what and whom is not always clear, but the idea of being representative is a *sine qua non* for the social scientist. The work of the scientist must be reproducible, not an easy task in the nature of social science, but the claim that the work is science implies that it could be replicated, giving the same results if all conditions were the same.

The criminologist takes several people, or large numbers, teases out the similarity of conditions, isolates the patterns of repeated factors, and makes a presentation from which conclusions are drawn. The writer, or for that matter the painter, has studied humanity in a unique but unsystematic manner. He has learned about the world by living in it, absorbing and illuminating its appearances and realities, a technique not foreign to the social scientists, particularly those influenced by the work in Chicago when that university's ascendancy was undisputed and those who have adopted the less empirical, more qualitative approach of participant-observation. But the social scientist, even when venturing forth to learn about the world by living in it rather than by merely asking questions about it, so often naively believing in the truth of the respondents, does so with training for this task, with previous systematic study of the people whom he is researching, with knowledge of former studies and how they were conducted, and with an obligation to test what he finds by comparison of his results with related and competitive theory and research.

It might appear, at first glance, that the scientist has the superior method, and if he has not revealed truths as penetrating as those limned by the artist, perhaps science has not attracted thinkers as great as those who have utilized literature as a method for dissemination of their thought. Such an answer is doubtful. Yet if the minds have been as great, and the method superior, why is it difficult to find criminologists with insights into human nature comparable to those of Shakespeare and Dostoevsky? Actually, the superiority of one method of perceiving or presenting information should not concern us, for both methods, in the hands of profound thinkers, are necessary, each for different reasons, to yield complementary portraits and the understandings that can be derived therefrom.

Artists and novelists on the one hand, criminologists and related behavioral scientists on the other, use different means to arrive at their results, different methods to explain them. The method of presentation favored by the artist is metaphor. The meanings are implicit, and they became more so with the development of literary style and the evolution of the novel as an art form. The method favored by the behavioral scientist is that of explication, and if this is the abandonment of metaphor, then it is difficult to sustain the concept of social science, whether sociology or any other, as an art form.

Dostoevsky, Faulkner, Conrad, and such other writers not described in these essays as Kafka, Camus, and Genet portray for us people, social worlds, events, and circumstances from which we readers can deduce significant social meanings. The criminologist locates a representative sample, the novelist creates a representative character.

"In Dostoevsky's *Crime and Punishment,* based upon his own experiences with police and prison," writes Nisbet, "Raskolnikov is not only a highly memorable individual but also the image of a class or type Dostoevsky was fascinated by."[7] Then Nisbet proceeds to contend that with Raskolnikov and numerous other characters from Balzac, Tolstoi, Dickens, and others, "we are dealing with a distinct, unforgettable *individual.*"[8] But they are individuals who are also social types. To emerge as an individual is a necessity for the success of the novel as an art form, but were the individual not a social type, he would represent only himself and fail to give the reader a vision of humanity, as conceived by the author. Dostoevsky, like Conrad, Defoe, and others, chooses these individuals to be representative. The criminologist would not be permitted such liberties. He would have to establish their representativeness.

In the instance of interpretation, both novelists and criminologists have to be speculative. The portraits, characters, events, and settings of the novelist are like the data that the criminologist uses, but while the novelist offers only intuition to justify his choice, the sociologist cites statistical formulations and a body of material that has been culled from what has come to be called methodology. The criminologist brings forth the data from which he draws conclusions, but there is nothing in the data that demands those specific conclusions. Other conclusions might be equally justified, and sometimes are, with canons of scientific method, rules of induction and deduction, concepts of parsimony and falsifiability that the social scientist must fall back on to justify his interpretations. The novelist draws no conclusions, in the sense in which the scientist deliberately organizes his data into logical structures that invite succinct summary statements. The literary artist presents us with no statistics on per capita income and crime rates to ponder, but may describe the staggering difficulties the poor and the guilt-ridden must face in coping with mere survival.

The writer of fiction embodies his ideas with characters whose life rhythms punctuate the social reality of statistics with an immediacy and a poignancy unsuited to a scientific monograph. To depict reality solely in terms of equations and documents—and *solely* is not what the responsible social scientist does, whatever stereotypical images the public may hold of him—represents an insolence and a futility if the point of research is, after all, to communicate ideas. The insights the artist may bring to his project do not merely dramatize reality but inform us as well and deepen our knowledge of the world and of humanity. For example, Raskolnikov is not a cipher of a political creed, the creature of a polemicist. He does not transform his outrage at social injustice into terrorism but instead he crushes the skull of a helpless old woman. Even here, the deed, for all its abjectness, comes through as understandable. Dostoevsky shows Raskolnikov as a victim of a callous and insensitive social system, but he is in no way exculpated because he was victim before he became victimizer.

Though the modes of work of the literary artist and scientist are distinctive, these blur before the deepest and most fundamental goals of each: to make the world meaningful and comprehensible. The artist, whatever his medium, and the scientist, whatever his discipline, provide order to the world in such ways as to attribute logic and meaning to it. Both set in motion new kinds of associations between ideas and emotions and in so doing not only enhance our grasp of the world of men and women but add to it new dimensions in the experience of living.

In both art and science, the interpretations are inherent in the work, but the artist stops to allow readers and critics to continue without his aid. Both artist and sociologist can be said to be offering data; and while they differ in whether they will make explicit their interpretations, in neither instance should the interpretations be confused with the data.

Lord Jim, abandoning a ship and several hundred people to their fate, is an individual, and if he were not, readers would never be caught up in his sorrows or concerned about his destiny. He is only one person, but the fact that Conrad has chosen this person to portray, and not another, is itself a statement about that writer's involvement with human issues. The moment that readers visualize Jim as a sailor who deserted his ship, they have ceased to confine him to the status of the individual and have begun to ponder human frailty, indecision, and the meaning of lost honor. How representative Jim is of humanity, or even of a part of it, only the reader can decide: it is fundamentally a question of whether Conrad's vision of the world is a profoundly convincing one. But when criminologists describe a group of prisoners, convicted burglars, or victims of violent crime, the readers know, or are at least supposed to know, how many such people have been seen, how they have been studied, what questions were asked, what observations made, what information elicited. The representativeness of the sample can be challenged, in a manner somewhat similar to the challenge that some would make as to whether Jim, Meursault, and Temple Drake represent more than themselves.

Thus the same problems are raised in the two cultures, but not by the same people and not in the same way. What seems to be occurring here is that two groups of thinkers are each bringing their own methods and techniques to focus on the same phenomenon. In different historical periods when great philosophical conceptions of humanity and the world became popular, science and literature reflected these trends in their approaches and productions. In writing about the Romantic movement, Edmund Wilson in *Axel's Castle* observed that in the seventeenth and eighteenth centuries artists and scientists "examined human nature dispassionately, in the same lucid and reasonable spirit, to find the principles on which it worked. Thus, the theories of the physicists were matched by the geometrical plays of Racine and the balanced couplets of Pope."[9]

But Racine was not a Newton, nor was Newton a poet. In the problems to which these essays are addressed, we would not say that Dostoevsky was a great criminologist, or a criminologist at all, or that his contemporaries who were studying crime were artists, but only that some novelists and criminologists had profound insights into the nature of crime and the criminal, attained through dissimilar methods, usually without each other's aid, and often arriving at mutually consistent conclusions.

There are, then, two portraits, or types of portraits, as Nisbet would contend. But unlike Nisbet, I prefer not to see sociology as an art form (ironically, this statement is itself a metaphor) or the novelist as a social scientist, but to regard the two as complementary observers and thinkers, elaborating on the same aspects of the human condition but utilizing different techniques to attain the same goals: to make the human experience more comprehensible and meaningful.

The alienation of these two cultures from each other is certainly not complete and total, and one need not resort to the example of Freud to be convinced of that. The works of sociology not infrequently quote, as examples and illustrations, from novels, the better to elaborate on abstract themes: from Sinclair Lewis, for one, to depict the nature of small-town American life in the 1920s, and especially its enforced and devitalizing conformity; from Kafka, to demonstrate the meaning and nature of bureaucracy; from Dickens, on social class and poverty in nineteenth-century England; from Dostoevsky's *Brothers Karamazov,* on power. And others. The American muckrakers included journalists and novelists—Lincoln Steffens, Ida Tarbell, Stephen Crane, Theodore Dreiser, Upton Sinclair—who portrayed a sector of society and various types of social problems, and sociologists have learned from them. Without the body of their works, who knows where sociology would be today. But let us not exaggerate: the impact has not been overwhelming.

Nor are novelists immune from the influence of the social scientist. A few have gone to the sociologists for their source material. For the most part, these have been among the minor writers, Marquands and not Joyces. That the great writers have drawn from psychology and psychoanalysis while contributing to the development of those fields only highlights the potential in a similarly symbiotic relationship with criminology.

The world has not been entirely impoverished by the gap between the two cultures, for in a more general sense, and in a variety of direct and indirect ways, knowledge accumulated by social scientists and expressed in their visions of the world has strong influence on literature. Over the past hundred years, Freud and Marx may have been the two prime examples of social thinkers who deeply affected the world of letters, but many others can be named: Charles Darwin, the Webbs, Lenin, and probably even more Trotsky, Gunnar Myrdal, György Lukács, David Riesman, Frantz Fanon, and perhaps the name of a criminologist might be found were the list lengthened sufficiently.

The bridges between the two cultures may be tenuous, constituting a fragile and inadequate connection, and it would seem to me that it is the world of criminology, not the world of letters, that has suffered. For Dostoevsky, who cannot properly be described as a criminologist, was nonetheless one of the most profound thinkers on crime and punishment, on suffering and redemption, whose creative work could enrich all of criminology, as it did the thinking of Freud, if criminologists would study it.

The links and ties will not be established by someone putting together a book—useful for other reasons though it might be—in which one of the many vivid passages in *Crime and Punishment* is placed side by side with similar passages from other important works on related subjects, to illustrate whatever it is meant to illustrate: remorse, techniques for justifying one's transgressions, thoughts of a man immediately prior to or after the commission of a terrible crime. Rather, precisely because the novel as an art form does not make it necessary, or even permissible, to draw conclusions from "the data" (that is, from individual characters and their experiences) in the manner of criminologists, Dostoevsky's work is most useful for hermeneutic purposes. What is the message of this book about humanity, truth, Christ, transgression, rebirth? The imposing body of such interpretations in works of literary critics (the "literary intellectuals," as Snow called them) stands in sharp contrast to their almost complete absence in criminology. It is out of concern about this contrast that the present essays were written.

The basic premise here, then, is that the literary images of crime and sin, punishment and retribution, expiation and atonement, are often as illuminating as those conveyed to us by criminologists, if not more so. They cannot be ignored by those who, in the pursuit of their investigations into this aspect of humanity in their own systematic and scientific manner, are seeking to reach an understanding of complex and anxiety-provoking issues. There is nothing inevitable about the gap between the two cultures. If anything, these essays are an attempt to bridge the polemical fiction of the two cultures and seek to show that the bifurcated approaches of the literary artist and social scientist are not irreconcilable.

The implicit claim running throughout the analysis is that the issues of crime, sin, redemption, and atonement need not necessarily be conceived in terms of either literary metaphors or scientific idioms. Rather, the expression and elucidation of these themes is greatly enhanced in terms of a network of concepts borrowing freely from both literary and scientific genres. Following the work of some twentieth-century philosophers, such as Wittgenstein, Russell, and, later, the other "ordinary language" analysts, it is possible to speak of varieties of human action without reducing them to the language of behaviorism or the sometimes impenetrable discourses of other scientific disciplines.

The method of analysis developed by the linguistic school tends to show that human action, including criminal actions and events, depends on more than one "language-game." The behavioral and social scientific discourses constitute only one of these games, guided by specific rules which define "behavior" as something observable and logically connected with other empirical parameters. Yet, despite the power and prestige of these idioms, the word *behavior* and the concepts it represents and symbolizes do not exhaust the meaning of the word *action*. Within the scientific paradigms, the term *behavior* commits its users to speak of "contingencies," "control," "deterrence," "incapacitation," and who knows what other terms, still undreamed of at this time. Eliminated from the scientific discourse are perfectly intelligible ideas and concepts concerning beliefs, desires, hopes, and ambitions that belong to another "language-game."

Undoubtedly some ideas from one language-game can be translated into another. Nevertheless, each mode of analysis with its special ontological base and assumptions has its own coherence and structure which is not always congenial and receptive to ideas and information emanating from other systems of thought. Such ideas as conditioning, aversion, reinforcement, deterrence, and rehabilitation, making up the vocabulary of contemporary criminological research, must remain "translations" in ordinary language systems and thereby suffer a loss of meaning. But what about fear, guilt, violence, remorse, hatred, and self-hatred? These notions reside in another idiom having more kinship with ethical and political questions than with the behavioristic languages of the sciences. Science and technology may lead to a set of policies, but not to moral perspectives. Scientific "grammars" of action do not have a monopoly on meaningfulness and coherence, and a retreat into them as the sole means of understanding, discussing, and coping with crime would be disastrous because, among other things, the scientific enterprise would lose its breadth should it deprive itself of opportunities to cross-fertilize with art and humanism.

The word *literature* has a double meaning. In one sense it refers to belles lettres and in another to the accumulated scientific writings on any subject. The former is literary, the latter almost never so, and on the subjects of crime and punishment, both literatures are vast. As prose, literature in the literary sense, developed in forms of tale, story, or novel, showed an early interest in crime but went off in at least three different directions. One of these was the novel of the rogue, an often delightful creature whose peregrinations we follow, whose capers amuse us, even when the acts themselves are violations of the law. The rogues were central characters in many of the picaresque novels, and Tom Jones represents, as much as does any single character, this type of fictional person. In more recent times, André Gide delighted readers with Lafcadio (in *Lafcadio's Adventures*, also translated as *The Caves of the Vatican*), and Thomas Mann with Felix Krull.

If the rogue is a transgressor, his sins are small. Raskolnikov is no Tom Jones, and Conrad was dealing with problems far different from those that engaged Fielding. We can only laugh at Felix Krull, or laugh with him, thief though he is, especially when the woman who seduces him, begging in vain for masochistic treatment at his hands, finds that she can receive this only by his stealing more from her. In the picaresque novel the protagonist was more hero than antihero; although he was a scoundrel, he was more a rascal or a wastrel than a criminal. His actions amuse and titillate the reader, they do not appall and outrage. If they are transgressions, they are minor ones in a world of abundant enormities.

In another direction entirely, often traced to Edgar Allan Poe, criminality in literature became a source of novels of suspense. These were mystery stories, sometimes macabre, and in Europe this literary strand went off in the direction of the Gothic novel, more somber than suspense-laden and designed to fill the reader with an eerie chill of terror. In France the mystery was called *le roman policier,* and some have classified *Crime and Punishment* in such a category. However, the difference is too great to permit the mystery novel and the fiction that delves into the mind of the criminal to be categorized as one. In the former, the reader is not left in suspense with regard to the meanings of human action as an abstraction; the wonderment, so often contrived, is over what those actions were and who committed them. It is a genre which, on some rare occasions, overlaps great literary treatments of crime, particularly when there is uncertainty as to whether or not the protagonist will be apprehended. For example, the "whodunit" element is not entirely absent from Faulkner; it is simply unimportant to an appreciation of his work. In a powerful novel like Richard Wright's *Native Son,* the reader is never left in doubt as to whether Bigger is the murderer. There is an entirely different kind of suspense involving how the memory of the event will weigh upon him, how it will motivate him in his actions during the hours and days that follow the murder, and whether he will justify the act and find inner peace.

Aside from the picaresque novel and the mystery, then, one is left with a huge legacy of works that illuminate, certainly as profoundly as the criminological literature, the propensity and capacity of humans to sin and to err, and their search for redemption and expiation.

Out of this vast library, I have chosen six characters who seem to me most significant in shedding light on this important aspect of the human condition and of social life. The reader may cavil at my choices, as one may also do at some of my interpretations. It is difficult to undertake a task of this sort, many would argue, and omit Mr. K., the victim of society, who does not know the nature of his transgression, cannot gain entry to the presence of those who will judge him, but accepts his guilt and faces his executioner. Or Meursault, the nonconformist, who killed and paid with his life, but who would hardly have been prosecuted or would certainly have been given only a slight penalty had he not shown indifference at his mother's funeral and contempt for the world of absurdity around him. Perhaps Mann's von Aschenbach belongs among these characters, symbolizing the decline of Western civilization, reaching for its lost and youthful vitality that can never be recovered, and in so doing displaying a perversity, a fatal flaw, that will lead to downfall and death in plague-ridden Venice. There might be room here for Mrs. Hutchinson, from Shirley Jackson's story "The Lottery," the chance victim of human cruelty, of man's inhumanity to man, who was so ready to be one of the offenders and who protests the unfairness of the violence only because *she* is the selected victim, not because it is morally wrong. Certainly criminology can be enriched by an analysis of such characters as Stephen Crane's Maggie, Richard Wright's already-mentioned Bigger, and Theodore Dreiser's social-climbing Clyde Griffiths, who hesitates for a moment as he brings about the death of his pregnant girlfriend, in a manner not without parallel when one examines Lord Jim. Or there is Queenie, the creation of Jean Genet, who represents, in the analysis of the criminologist Shoham, the concept of salvation through pollution, salvation through the gutters.[10]

It appeared to me that, if a small number of fictional characters were to be studied, the group selected here constituted a range useful in depicting a diversity of approaches to crime and transgression, suffering and atonement, redemption and expiation.

Raskolnikov is his own justification. His importance in this literature is unchallenged; to omit him would be to overlook Oedipus in a study of incest. He represents the depiction of a criminal who creates his own justification; of the idea that in the crime is found the punishment; that the first victim of each transgressor is the offender himself; and that each human being, no matter to what depths he has sunk, can like Lazarus rise from the dead. Moll Flanders prefigures an entire genre of criminological literature, occupies an important place in the development of the novel as the first major criminal protagonist who is not a delectable rogue, and illustrates the theme of repentance even if, in my interpretation, it is flawed because she is not a penitent.

Jean Valjean is the central character in a work that is a hallmark in the literature of social protest. I wish that Valjean had more human foibles, that he were somewhat short of saintliness and perfection, that he had committed some acts that I might consider transgressions. If this were so, the hundreds of pages of his haunted life might be more meaningful. Nevertheless, he symbolizes more than any other character in fiction the social theme that poverty creates evil, and the sociological theme that imprisonment deepens the schisms that divide convicts from the rest of humanity. His is the story of one who steals for that oft-cited reason, to obtain a loaf of bread, and the novel poignantly portrays both the relentless pursuit of an exconvict (in this instance justified by the fact that he is a fugitive) and the unyielding spirit of goodness that cannot be broken in the face of difficulties and adversities.

If I had no other justification, I would simply state that as a matter of personal preference I have chosen the remaining three characters, Lord Jim, Ethan Frome, and Temple Drake (the last from Faulkner's *Sanctuary* and *Requiem for a Nun*) because they are from four novels that I strongly favor and that I have returned to on many occasions. These are characters with whom I have lived, and I have shared the sufferings of the first two. Lord Jim, for all the controversy over the meaning of his life and his death, may be as profound an example of the search for redemption as one can locate in literature. Ethan Frome is not engaged in such a search. Rather, he is the symbol of suffering and atonement, of resignation to the fact that only death can relieve him of the burden of living. And Temple Drake, in an interpretation which may not be shared by many, is an outstanding example of redemption *manquée,* an unredeemed and irredeemable individual.

In their own ways, and they are different ways, the six characters offer us a spectrum of transgression. Their crimes do not have equal enormity (and of Frome, there may be question as to whether there was what can properly be called a crime), but their activities arose out of life patterns that approach universality, and all bring to the fore questions of responsibility that the individual assumes, or from which he seeks vainly to escape, for the consequences of his deeds. From these six characters we can learn, surely as well as from the greatest of criminologists or from the most representative sample subjected to rigorous statistical analysis, why people commit acts that are morally reprehensible, and what hope there is, if any, for redemption, expiation, atonement, forgiveness, and rebirth. These are among the most important problems of our age, and in fact of all ages.

NOTES

1. C. P. Snow, *The Two Cultures and the Scientific Revolution* (New York: Cambridge University Press, 1959), p. 10.

2. Ibid., p. 11.

3. Gilbert Geis, "Jeremy Bentham," in Hermann Mannheim, ed., *Pioneers in Criminology,* 2nd ed. (Montclair, N.J.: Patterson Smith, 1972), p. 60.

4. Marvin E. Wolfgang, "Cesare Lombroso," in Mannheim, ed., *Pioneers in Criminology,* p. 287.

5. Robert Nisbet, *Sociology as an Art Form* (New York: Oxford University Press, 1976).

6. References to the works of Sutherland, Chambliss, Klockars, and others are given in the essay on Moll Flanders in this volume.

7. Nisbet, *Sociology as an Art Form,* p. 69.

8. Ibid., p. 70, emphasis in original.

9. Edmund Wilson, *Axel's Castle: A Study in the Imaginative Literature of 1870 to 1930* (New York: Scribner, 1959), p. 3. (First published in 1931.)

10. S. Giora Shoham, *Salvation Through the Gutters: Deviance and Transcendence* (Washington, D.C.: Hemisphere, 1979).

2

RASKOLNIKOV
Man Is Condemned
to Be Free

It would be difficult to name a single work in literature that so completely embodies an entire theme as does Dostoevsky's *Crime and Punishment,* or a single character who recapitulates an entire type of human being as does Rodion Romanovich Raskolnikov. Not only is he a criminal and his act a crime, but he is literature's criminal and the murder of the pawnbroker and her half-sister is all crime. It is the genius of Dostoevsky that this is accomplished despite the unusual qualities of the character, his atypicality, and the fact that his one criminal act was not part of a continuing pattern (although it was not a complete departure from his character, either). If the term *criminal* is to be reserved for those who make a career, profession, or occupation of crime, as a Moll Flanders, or for those who remain, even for indefensible reasons, hunted, hounded, unforgiven, and forever labeled, as Jean Valjean, then Raskolnikov is hardly such a person. Not only is he none of these, he is not a stereotype; on the contrary, he negates all of the expectations one has of a person guilty of murder. Despite this extreme unrepresentative-

All quotations without notes are from Feodor Dostoevsky, *Crime and Punishment,* ed. George Gibian and trans. Jessie Coulson, Norton Critical Edition (New York: Norton, 1975). This translation first appeared in 1953; the quotations are reprinted by permission of Oxford University Press. All parenthetical phrases, ellipses, and italics appear in the original; bracketed words have been added by the author of this essay.

ness, he remains the symbol of the criminal in literature; and it is the penetration into Raskolnikov, unlike as he is to other offenders against the laws of humanity, that is the prime example of the successful exploration of the mind of the offender. Dostoevsky's novel is certainly the most ambitious of any single work of fiction dealing with the themes expressed in the title and the related ones of expiation, propitiation, redemption, and atonement.

A word about the title. It may have been only in a moment of pique that James Joyce remarked to his son George that *Crime and Punishment* "was a queer title for a book which contained neither crime nor punishment."[1] Yet, there is an insight here that is illuminated when one looks more carefully at the title, which in English may not completely capture the flavor that it has in Russian. George Gibian writes:

> The Russian word for "crime," in the title of the novel and elsewhere, is *prestuplenie,* from *pre* (across, trans-) and *stuplenie* (a stepping), so that etymologically it is similar to the English "transgression." The root meanings of "stepping across" some barrier, as both essential and analogous to the criminal, are played on in the text in a manner which is lost sight of in the translation, since our word "crime" does not have the same derivation. (P. 466)

And in fact this is not the story of a crime, a particular and specific double murder, or any other crime; it is the story of crime itself, and in it there unfolds the mind of the criminal and the punishment that he undergoes for his act. Crime, not the murder of two women, is the subject of the work, and there is no other landmark in the history of literature of which this can be said. What Dostoevsky has to say about the slayings themselves is almost incidental. They are the vehicle to enable the author to discuss crime and portray the criminal, and the tale is woven because this is a novel, not exposition. As a novel it proceeds on two levels simultaneously: one follows the sequence of events, conversations, activities, and occasionally omissions, and the other conveys the author's message about life, society, the human condition, and in many instances specifically about crime and the criminal mind.

The second part of the title is equally provocative. In one sense, there is a beauty in the message conveyed by the word *punishment,* for reasons primarily of omission. The novel devotes the last dozen or so pages, of almost five hundred, to Raskolnikov's years in prison. It is not an afterthought, but certainly an epilogue. So long as punishment is conceived of in its legal-political meaning, whether it be carried out by execution, whipping, confinement, excommunication, banishment, or even the mild levying of a fine, or through such informal social interactions as ostracism, ridicule, or general hostility, the title appears to be a misnomer. The novel hardly makes mention of these forces.

There appears to be gross imbalance, then, for *Crime and Punishment* is almost entirely about crime, ignoring punishment. If anything, Raskolnikov is treated with special kindness and forgiveness, even love, by the important persons around him after they discover that he is the murderer: by his sister, by his closest friend, Razumikhin, especially by Sonya, and one can even add by his mother, selflessly pretending to the last day of her life that she is ignorant of his imprisonment and the reasons for it.

It is Dostoevsky's message, almost his discovery, that it is not in its legal or social manifestations that true punishment is found, but in the inner turmoil, the self-flagellation, the regrets, the remorse, the grief of one whose guilt becomes too great to carry within. If this is not accepted, then the title loses its meaning. This is not to say that one is otherwise dealing with crime without punishment, because that would imply impunity, or freedom from social retaliation, which Raskolnikov does not receive. Rather, it would demonstrate a disproportionate emphasis on the crime rather than the punishment, and the justification of the first word of the title would hardly be extendable to the last.

So accustomed are we to thinking of this novel as *Crime and Punishment* that one stops and receives a new perspective when confronted with the fact that the Russian was translated in a somewhat different manner into French, Spanish, and other languages. In French, which was for the Russians of the nineteenth century the language of culture, the work is called *Crime et Châtiment*, the last word closely resembling the English *chastisement*.[2] Now, there is a word in French that corresponds to the English *punishment*, namely *punition*, and to the extent that words in different languages, except when used in a strictly scientific context, always have some nuances, tones, or flavors that make them less than interchangeable, seldom if ever expressing exactly the same thought, one must be struck by the interpretation of the character, treatment, and suffering of Raskolnikov when one conceives of the events that follow upon his crime as chastisement rather than punishment. Chastisement is a cleansing action, to make one chaste again by paying for one's unchaste acts; it is purification and expiation because one takes responsibility for one's own pollution. Punishment too is suffering and except in some instances where it is undeserved and unearned (not germane to this work), it comes as an answer to one's transgressions and for the responsibilities of one's wrongdoings.[3] Punishment, however, contains within it no implication that there will be a rebirth of good, that the evil can be paid for and expunged. The suffering is solely for the past misdeeds; it can be retributive and vengeful, rather than corrective; a hopeless dungeon, a tunnel that has no light and in which one wanders and breathes the dank air until rescued by death or set free, unchanged, ready to repeat one's wrongs. Chastisement offers hope; that is why the word is so often used for children, because it is a form of suffering inflicted on them so that they will learn and, being children, they are presumed to be in a moldable, malleable, learning state. The references in *Crime and Punishment* to Lazarus, who rose from the dead, the insistence by Raskolnikov that Sonya read to him the parable of Lazarus from the New Testament, and then the further insistence by Dostoevsky that her reading not be summarized in a sentence or two, but rather that this lengthy narrative be incorporated as part of his own text, is the indication of Dostoevsky's essentially hopeful view of humanity, and at the same time of Raskolnikov's need to share this view. No matter what one has done, one can rise again, but to do so it is necessary to admit that the act has been performed, to accept responsibility for it, and to understand the enormity of the evil inherent in it. There are no Christs to suffer and die on the cross for the sins of others, certainly not for your sins and mine, for one must die for one's own acts in order to be reborn, but rebirth is within the grasp of all persons.

In the view of Dostoevsky, the events that lead up to a criminal act are significant to the extent that crime, evil, and transgression are abstractions to be clarified, but they are not in themselves important as explanations of single acts. Crime like everything else has causes, and without failing to cite the sources of such causes in social conditions, from poverty and hunger to a climate of corruption and greed, Dostoevsky goes beyond such an emphasis, focusing rather on the manner in which a few individuals make use of, and are in turn used by, the social situations in which they are enmeshed. The motives for the murders of the pawnbroker and her half-sister are complex and ambiguous; in fact, the ambiguity assumes an eventual importance in its own right. However, the ways in which the reasons for committing the acts are handled in the mind of Raskolnikov, giving rise to the aura of ambiguity, serving as justifications, as mechanisms for the avoidance of responsibility, become crucial not only to him but to an understanding of him.

In Dostoevsky, humanity is redeemable, Lazarus does rise. Man is not inherently or innately evil, but each of us has a capacity for evil. It is in one's conduct, not in one's being or essence, that evil is located when the potential is translated into action.

Raskolnikov's significance is enhanced, in part at least, by the fact that fundamentally he is a likable, compassionate individual, and one who evokes this compassion in those who know him (the characters in the novel) and those who meet him (the readers of the novel). He is not an antihero who is the center of attention and for whom we start to applaud, sometimes despite ourselves, from the sidelines of life, or on the margins of a book. He is not a prototype for a protagonist with whom the author compels us, by the force of his literary skill, to align ourselves despite our own better judgment. Nor is he a lovable rogue of the sort that English literature gave us, particularly during the era of Fielding. Although he does not benefit monetarily from his crime—burying part of the loot, using another part to aid a family in need—Raskolnikov has not the slightest element of a Robin Hood in his makeup; he only finds useful the Robin Hood mentality or myth to give both *a priori* and *ex post facto* justification to the murders.

Therein lies one of Dostoevsky's many great strengths: he can succeed in separating the act from the man, by making the former grim, grisly, and in short both symbol and embodiment of evil, allowing for no mitigation, no extenuating circumstances, and yet portraying a human being who emerges as the actor who himself is not base. There are many far less attractive persons in Dostoevsky, both in this and in his other works, but they commit no crimes of the enormity of the double slaying. Faulkner's criminals evoke disgust in us, but Dostoevsky's evoke disgust, or more exactly revulsion, mainly in themselves. Raskolnikov is a fragile human, ready at any moment to collapse—he is fragile more than frail, for he has strengths, but they are actually outward displays of strength put forward the better to conceal, especially from himself, his fragility—and because all persons are fragile, separated from disintegration only by a hairline, one can relate to the man even though one cannot identify with his misdeeds.

He commits two murders, the second of which (later, this is to assume even greater importance in his suffering than the first) is unplanned. Even here, however, he cannot take refuge in a type of justification that criminal jurisprudence so often offers to those who commit crimes that they had had no intention to carry out and, in fact, had even sought to avoid. The first murder, the killing of the pawnbroker herself, could hardly have been more deliberate, more premeditated, and in the language of the courts, more filled with malice aforethought. When the sister Lizaveta enters the flat where the first murder had already taken place, and Raskolnikov is jolted by surprise—he had planned the act to take place at a time when she would not be present, not out of compassion for her but because her absence would simplify his task—he axes her to death as he had already done to the pawnbroker. What Dostoevsky thus creates is the perfect crime, not in the sense that the perpetrator cannot be apprehended and has left no clues, but perfect in that it symbolizes crime free from any of the justifications and excuses that, under other circumstances, diminish its evil content and serve to relieve the offender of at least part of his personal responsibility for its commission. The slaying of the pawnbroker in that sense is in complete juxtaposition to the stealing of the loaf of bread by Jean Valjean. That Raskolnikov can emerge and rise again is in and of itself a statement of Dostoevsky's affirmation of humanity; that Raskolnikov can be presented not in the degradation of Faulkner's Popeye, not in the mediocrity of Moll Flanders, not in the weakness of Lord Jim, but as the deliberate committer of the most heinous of offenses and at the same time as human and even humane, is a tribute to the genius of his creator and to the expression of the latter's view of the world.

One can contrast Raskolnikov with Kafka's Mr. K., for both suffer from the burden of the guilt that they carry within and that is imposed on them from without. But Raskolnikov knows why he is condemned to carry this burden, and his struggle is to find some method of justification to himself so that he can live without need for expiation. In *The Trial*, Mr. K. bears the burden of outer guilt, of prosecution by others, which he is ready to accept as deserved, but he is in constant ignorance of the reason for that prosecution. He knows that he must have committed a crime, because otherwise there would be no arrest and no trial, and he accepts his own guilt, but the nature of the crime itself is unknown to him, and unknowable. Raskolnikov's guilt acknowledges both his crime and his complicity in committing it, but his is a struggle against that guilt, an inner rage that expresses itself in a search for motivation that would give justification, if not in the eyes of others, then at least in his own.

There is a remarkable interweaving of cause, motivation, and rationalization in the murders carried out by Raskolnikov. The pawnbroker is killed for money: it is a crime of greed and of need. The killer is a poverty-stricken student who cannot bring himself to take further funds from his mother and sister. He sits in his desolate room and, half-starved, manages to survive on what he has borrowed from one source and begged from another and, most recently, from the meager proceeds of some personal treasures that he has pawned. There are other roads left for him, but he rejects them: he will not tutor young students any longer, for the entire process revolts him, it demeans him. Sometime earlier, he had written and had published anonymously (although he is not even aware that it has been published) an article on the rights of the more gifted sectors of humanity to rule, oppress, expropriate, and exterminate the less useful. The supermen in person-to-person activities have the same right as have the leaders of powerful nations: the stronger do not permit the weaker to stand in the way of destiny. It was to accomplish his human destiny that Napoleon caused the death of thousands or tens of thousands; this was history, progress, the burdens and privileges of the few. In similar manner, the talented may and in fact must sweep aside the parasites, the useless, the stupid, the mass of persons who stand in the way of the elect, the portion of humanity endowed with innate superiority. Of course, no society permits a few to set themselves above or outside the law, so that those who believe that they are chosen must carry out their illegal acts surreptitiously, but their higher intelligence enables them to understand the social good and the human necessity, or at least the justification, for their activities.

Here, then, are two forces: poverty and the lure of easy gold, and superior intelligence that reduces in his haughty mind the holder of that gold to "a vile, noxious insect," not a human being but a louse masquerading as human. The world will soon forget that she has lived, and she will be buried but not mourned, neither by Petersburg, Russia, nor the human race. Once he has chosen her as his victim, a choice made because of her vulnerability, her cash and other resources, and the ease with which the crime can apparently be effected, he can feel neither pity nor sorrow for her, not because this is outside the gamut of emotional responses of which he is capable, but because the justifications that he has already created require that he reduce her in his own mind to lower and lower status, that he see her as subhuman or dehumanized, particularly in contrast to himself. At this point, there is evidence that Raskolnikov detests himself, and in the language of a yet unborn psychoanalysis and psychology, he is projecting outward on a chosen victim the disgust that he harbors toward his own inner being.

The pawnbroker is to be swept aside, he reasons, because no ignorant parasite has the right to stand in the path of himself or one like him. He is the chosen, a status that he perceives through inner revelation. In historical perspective, one can say that Dostoevsky could have been writing about slavery and colonialism, and about the methods of the masters and the imperialists to justify their pillage, exploitation, and murder, although the closest he comes to extension of the superman thesis is to invoke the name of Napoleon on several occasions. Even more frightening, as one looks at the patterns of genocide of the twentieth century, is the terribly prophetic message of the superman and his freedom to kill.

It is only after the crime has been committed that the enormity of the act begins to take its toll of the perpetrator. Not immediately, for first he must escape from the scene, in which he nearly becomes trapped, and precisely because he has such excellent control of his senses (although he does make some minor errors, as people who have committed ostensibly unsolvable crimes so often do), he escapes apprehension at that moment. Carrying some money and several articles stolen from the victim, and with the axe that was his murder weapon hidden under his cloak, he manages to leave the locus of the crime. He returns the axe to its rightful owner and to its rightful place before its absence is noted. He is now free: free to suffer, free to condemn himself, free to be seized.

The punishment of Raskolnikov is about to begin. He is a person fraught with conflict and ambiguity, and he summarizes within himself what has so often been analyzed by forensic psychiatrists, criminologists, and psychoanalysts: he is living in constant dread that he will be caught, and at the same time only by being caught will he be able to feel liberated from the burden that he is carrying. He must confess, although the confession will be punishment and will bring it, but failure to confess—or, more concretely, denial—will be equally if not more oppressive. Caught in this dilemma of his own making, he becomes obsessed with the need to leave hints of his culpability wherever he goes, sometimes these clues being scattered without provocation, making them all the more noticeable, and at other times being drawn out of him, and finally he falls helplessly into a trap that he knows has been set for him. Through it all he suffers, and his suffering is enhanced, rather than reduced, whenever he imagines that he will escape from the net that surrounds him, and that his crime, or specifically his part in it, is not going to become public knowledge.

Yet it is not that Raskolnikov requires admiration from the world for having carried out the murder, or having done so too cleverly for the authorities to be able to seize him as the culprit. His problem is that he can receive no admiration from himself. The satisfaction, the self-gratification that he had expected, both from the crime and from the fruits of it, are not forthcoming. Instead of turning his hatred inward, he seizes all the more on his theory of superman, counting himself as one of the elect and the pawnbroker as nothing more than a louse that had to be exterminated. He clings to the ideology all the more because he believes in it all the less, for without it he is lost. Should he be bereft of his superman thesis, there is nothing left for him but to turn against himself, or so he believes at this stage of his life, in the days immediately following the murders. Like others suffering from the memories of their own immoralities, he becomes moralistic; there is nothing but condemnation for one suitor of his sister, and little else for another. Raskolnikov, however, is too profound a thinker to be confounded by his own double standards of morality; he sees through himself, is aware of his own motivations, is victimized by his own self-oppression.

The punishment that Raskolnikov suffers, not at the hands of the officials and legal authorities but in terms of inner torture, begins at the time of the murders or a few hours after, when he has escaped from the scene. It is a torture that eventually leads him to enter the station house, although the evidence against him is weak and he is not about to be arrested, and to announce softly, brokenly, distinctly, "It was I who killed the old woman and her sister, Lizaveta, with an axe, and robbed them" (p. 450). His punishment will continue, however, even when he is in prison, and will only be alleviated when he has found inner peace through acknowledging responsibility for his act and recognizing the evil in it. For Raskolnikov, as for Dostoevsky— who had spent several years in Siberia, in prison and in exile—there is a harshness inflicted on prisoners, but it is not through receiving one's just deserts that one is redeemed. Redemption comes through acceptance of responsibility for one's actions, and suffering thereupon begins to diminish, not to accumulate.

Raskolnikov rises to the highest levels of human expiation precisely because his suffering comes from within. That he never admits repentance, does not appear contrite, and, even after his confession and imprisonment, is still clinging to his belief in a superman concept that offers him a spurious though ever more tenuous exoneration, is nothing more than further evidence of how strongly the regret is burning within him. Both to the world without and to himself, a façade must be presented: superiority because he has confronted himself with his own moral inferiority, haughtiness because he is filled with revulsion against self, anger against others so that it can be deflected lest it travel against himself. Tortured and tormented, his entry into the police station to surrender and announce that he is the murderer they are seeking is a relief, not only in the sense that the confessional of the Catholic church and the outpourings to the analyst are cathartic, but because the period of most severe punishment, that inflicted on himself, has been resolved (or almost entirely so, for there are some problems to be faced before expiation can be completed).

The years in Siberia are not easy ones. He is a loner, the godless outsider, rejected by other prisoners, unable either to become one of them or to be contented without being part of their circles. There are no simple contrasts between the days following the murder and those in prison; the latter are painted as serene in order to emphasize that punishment in its fullest sense was the inner turmoil that existed in the earlier period. Siberia is hell, it is suffering and torture, physical, mental, and emotional deprivation, and sexual too, although this never enters into Dostoevsky's explicit descriptions, so that the contrast with the postmurder days is a subtle one. Yet it is inescapable that the earlier period is when the true punishment holds sway.

If this interpretation is accepted, it might be argued that the atypicality of Raskolnikov is a defect, for Dostoevsky is not describing crime as an abstraction and generalization but as an act committed by a human being capable of carrying out the act and following it with depths of contrition. What can this tell us about the criminal who robs with impunity, mocks his victims, repeats his evil deeds, and enjoys their fruits? It is not necessary to contend that he is a less typical criminal than is Raskolnikov (he is probably much more so), or to claim that, far beneath the surface and in the depths of the unconscious, he too is suffering but does not know it. To find the truths about the human condition in Dostoevsky, no such devices are necessary, and any would be flawed. One need only interpret his message that Raskolnikov represents and summarizes the capacity of humanity in four related directions: first, to commit evil deeds for which there is no moral mitigation; second, to rationalize and seek to justify one's own activities, both before and after the crime; third, to suffer and repent because the germ of human goodness is ever-present; and finally, to rise again through complete expiation.

There are millions of humans who do not perform the first of these, the evil in itself, but humanity has a capacity for it, even the best of people. A few carry out such acts, and they are the criminals; most persons do not, they are the rest, but they are born to walk on the brink of such performance, and if all persons, unlike Cain, have not murdered, they have all, like Adam, fallen.

Had the crime been less serious, had there been any justification, had Raskolnikov shown some glimmer of mercy during its commission, had there been some provocation, he could not summarize the capacity for evil in humanity as he does. More than that, the ability to rise would be diluted if he were not at the lowest possible level of degradation. He comprises, then, man's fatal flaw and his greatest hope, combined in one person. The link between the fall and the rise is punishment (which is why it is so accurate to call it chastisement, a purification of a polluted spirit). It is not and cannot be the punishment of the torture chamber, of the whipping post and the swinging rack, of the galleys of France where Jean Valjean so long slaved, or of that peculiar developed-in-America institution, the prison. These are all there, for without them even the most hopeful and optimistic viewers of the human scene would find it difficult to retain a vision of an ongoing society, but the greatest punishment is that which an individual inflicts upon himself. Some escape from such torment, and some give it to themselves undeservedly. But those who fall into the ways of a Raskolnikov without suffering his fate, a fate at his own hands and in the mirror of the eyes of Sonya, Dunya, Razumikhin, and others whom he loved, are persons for whom there is nonetheless hope (much as they might scorn and reject it). There is hope because Raskolnikov demonstrates the human capacity for rebirth.

This theme of inner suffering and self-inflicted punishment is articulated by Dostoevsky in his own notes about his novel, in which he writes that in *Crime and Punishment* he hints at the thought "that [legal] punishment for a crime frightens a criminal much less than we think [the lawmakers in part] because the criminal himself [morally] demands it."[4] (The bracketed words are in the original, indicating that they were added by Dostoevsky after the writing of the notes themselves.)

From the moment Raskolnikov plans the murder, he finds it loathsome and is filled with self-revulsion at the realization that he is entertaining such thought. Yet he does not cease to make meticulous plans to carry it out. He visits the pawnbroker not to pawn another item but to case her place, watch her carefully, making mental note of where she places her purse and keys, where she keeps the most valuable pawned items, how he will be able quickly to get to her safe boxes. The act of murder is not impulsive, impetuous, or in any way irresistible; he knows where he will obtain the axe, how he will be able to return it, at what time the sister will not be present so that there will be no need to silence a witness while killing a victim. At the same time, he cannot believe that he is seriously planning to carry out the crime.

The question of motivation is never resolved: does Raskolnikov murder for the money (which he does not use, but that is another story, for he did not foresee the inner impediments that would prevent him from spending it for his own pressing needs) or to establish the intellectual superiority of a part of the species with whom he identified? The problem is not resolved by Dostoevsky because there is ambiguity in Raskolnikov himself. He is impelled by the money and the desperation of his poverty, while at the same time the superman theory requires validation by the commission of a crime permitted only to the elect. Thus, the restraints that would normally make it impossible to kill are neutralized, if not entirely broken, by the ability of and the need for justifications. His incapacity or unwillingness to dispose of the money except in a manner that will not benefit himself, at times altruistically and at other times irresponsibly, serves the purpose both of assisting in having himself apprehended, something toward which he is working without conscious realization, and of alleviating the inner guilt by not profiting from the fruits of the crime, by having part of the benefits of it go to some poor and deserving innocent others while the remainder is hidden and untouched.

Rodion Romanovich Raskolnikov has the attributes of a good man, and without them he would not be the most important literary image of the criminal that creative genius has offered. He is a faithful and loving son and brother. This love for the two women in his family is not a mockery of mankind, it is not a caricature to show that he and others like him are hypocrites whose benevolence is only a mask for their malevolence, but just the reverse. Behind the most evil deed of man there lies a person capable of goodness.

Even after he has committed his murders and has not yet been apprehended, he insults Luzhin, who has come to him as his sister Dunya's suitor. There is a tragicomic irony here, or at least as close to the comic as anything in so somber a work can be: here is the most reprehensible of murderers telling another man that he is unworthy to enter his family, and the other departs, overbearing and angry, determined that he will press his suit on the sister the following day when the impertinent brother is absent.

Nor do Raskolnikov's qualities of faithfulness end there: he is a loyal friend to Razumikhin, there is love between the two, and when he finds himself strongly hinting to Razumikhin that he has committed a terrible crime, it is out of a wish to spare his friend and not himself that he cannot quite articulate the truth; it is not self-pity that emerges from this scene, it is Raskolnikov's profound regret that he is causing such distress to a beloved friend.

Such qualities notwithstanding, the one great crime of his life is not out of keeping with Raskolnikov's character. It is not an accident, something that happened to happen, a senseless act that exploded within him as if a demon had seized him. He has not only carefully planned it, he has already laid the groundwork for the intellectual rationalization of it, and he has a capacity for doing this (as proven by the fact that he does do it) and for doing similar acts of an evil nature. Even before he has killed Alëna and Lizaveta, when he first hears about the pursuit of Dunya by Luzhin, he is intensely bitter, "and if he had chanced to meet Mr. Luzhin at that moment [of reading the letter from his mother], he would have felt like murdering him," Dostoevsky writes (p. 35). Were it not for this and similar although less explicit passages, the message of the author would be quite different, for he would be narrating the tragedy of one who, on a single occasion, failed, not one who had a chronic capacity for such failings. There is evil in the hearts and minds of all persons, because they are part of the human race, evil epitomized by the least excusable of all crimes, murder. If Raskolnikov is to recapitulate for us mankind's fall and rise, then the act to which he falls cannot be a departure from his self.

The guilt that follows him after the murders is already present in the planning stage, and it is both punishing and at the same time serves as an attempt, unsuccessful as it turns out, to stay his hand. He is a man in conflict, unsure of what he is doing or wants to do, but not lacking the mental capacity to know right from wrong and to control his course of action. In full possession of his faculties, he is nevertheless the center of the battleground between Jehovah and Satan for control of his own soul. If he were not so devoid of sexual drive or motivation, he would be Freud's superego and id engaged in full battle with each other, or Schopenhauer's will and idea. The inner conflict of Raskolnikov, however, is more on a moral plane, and in that sense theological, although devoid of supernaturalism and faith. When he learns that at precisely seven o'clock Lizaveta will be away from the flat where she resides with Alëna so that the old woman will then be alone and hence will be easier prey for him, he has moved that much closer to perpetrating the murder. It is now only one day away. The student who now finds that his crime can be carried out with greater probability of impunity, less possibility of interruption than he had dared to hope, is not joyous, for he finds himself moving inexorably toward the commission of his crime.

> It was only a few steps farther to his lodging. He went in like a man condemned to death. He did not reason about anything, he was quite incapable of reasoning, but he felt with his whole being that his mind and will were no longer free, and that everything was settled, quite finally. (P. 53)

That Raskolnikov will indeed proceed to murder is at this point inevitable. He has relinquished his freedom, has decided that there is a destiny and that he is caught up in it. In so doing, he is giving himself no choice, is sealing his fate, is becoming a prisoner of his own past, and is building up a new rationale that he will use to excuse if not to justify the crime he is now surely going to commit: namely, that he is not a free man able to refrain from committing it. It is not a line of reasoning with which he can ever be reconciled, soothing as it might have been, for Dostoevsky, perhaps the greatest of the literary existentialists, himself rejects this. The lesson of Raskolnikov is clear: Man is condemned to be free.

Condemnation to freedom appears to be a paradox, no more than a play on words, but its meanings are penetrated both by Dostoevsky and by the criminal he creates. There is no cop-out for acts of evil, no mitigating events, no predecessing causes that throw a blanket of determinism over life and thus relieve the actor of responsibility for his acts. Each person must accept what he does and the consequences thereof: there is no such justification in the arsenal of human evaluation of the conduct of ourselves and others as having "mind and will" that are "no longer free." Nothing is ever settled, certainly not "quite finally," at least not until after it has occurred, whether it be the behavior of a saint or the basest of sinners.

Later, and still before the murders, Raskolnikov overhears two men speaking in a tavern, and indeed their talk concerns the pawnbroker Alëna Ivanovna and her half-sister Lizaveta. A student and a young officer are heatedly discussing them at the very next table. A conversation of this nature would ordinarily strain the credibility of a reader, for coincidences of such magnitude, in which two people are speaking loudly and heatedly about the justifications of a murder that the listener is himself contemplating and that he has confided to no one, go beyond the licenses, poetic and other, given to a novelist. It would be easy to explain that the conversation never existed, that in his already tormented mind he is hearing it but that it is actually a fantasy in whose reality he believes, but there is no evidence that Dostoevsky intended such an interpretation. Rather, the student and officer are placed at the next table by Dostoevsky so that Raskolnikov can see each of them as his double, or more exactly, each is a double of one of his two warring selves. They are his mirror, the mirror of his mind, and they are offering him an opportunity to hear from without the conversations that are going on within him. At one point:

> "I swear I could kill that damned old woman and rob her, without a single twinge of conscience," exclaimed the student hotly.
> The officer laughed again, but Raskolnikov found this so strange that he shuddered. (P. 55)

The student is quick to explain that he has only been joking. This is the superego dismissing the murderous drive within as something not worthy of serious consideration, to be shrugged off as no more than a joke. The absolution of self, however, takes but a fraction of a moment, is held on to for only a few words, and the student has returned to a justification of the murder (after assuring the soldier that he will not and would not commit it), and in so doing he utilizes the very line of thought that is taking place in the mind of the listening student, Raskolnikov:

> "I was joking just now, of course, but look here: on the one hand you have a stupid, silly, utterly unimportant, vicious, sickly old woman, no good to anybody, but in fact quite the opposite, who doesn't know herself why she goes on living, and will probably die tomorrow without any assistance. Do you understand what I am saying?"
> "Oh, I follow you," answered the officer, earnestly studying his companion's vehemence.
> "Listen, then. On the other hand you have new, young forces running to waste for want of backing, and there are thousands of them, all over the place. A hundred, a thousand, good actions and promising beginnings might be forwarded and directed aright by the money that old woman

destines for a monastery; hundreds, perhaps thousands, of existences might be set on the right path, scores of families saved from beggary, from decay, from ruin and corruption, from the lock hospitals—and all with her money! Kill her, take her money, on condition that you dedicate yourself with its help to the service of humanity and the common good: don't you think that thousands of good deeds will wipe out one little, insignificant transgression?" (Pp. 55–56)

It is now clear that this is an internal dialogue, taking place within Raskolnikov. He is the student, but he is also the officer, listening, assenting, finding it more and more difficult to marshal an argument against what is being put forth. It is not that Raskolnikov is imagining this conversation, but that Dostoevsky is transforming the protagonist into two doubles and confronting him with both of them. Raskolnikov can do no more than listen while they argue over the fate of his own inner selves: one is the student who would justify murder, the other is law and authority, the embodiment of official morality.

The student is quick to protect himself. Would you kill the old woman with your own hands, the officer asks, and the other replies: "Of course not! For the sake of justice, I . . . This is not a question of me at all!" (P. 56).

Again, as he had upon accidentally learning that Lizaveta would be absent at a given hour the following day, Raskolnikov seizes upon the conversation that he has overheard to escape responsibility for what he is planning to do:

This casual public-house conversation had an extraordinary influence on the subsequent development of the matter, as if there were indeed something fateful and foreordained about it. (P. 57)

He is moving closer to entrapment in the crime by the growing renunciation of the freedom to choose, by the emphasis on destiny, of something fateful and foreordained. But he is not more reconciled to the murder, in fact less:

One noticeable peculiarity characterized all the final decisions he arrived at in this affair: the more settled they were, the more hideous and absurd they appeared in his eyes. In spite of his agonizing internal struggles he could never throughout the whole time believe for one instant in the practicability of his schemes. (P. 59)

A sort of Freudian dialectic can be constructed from this: the more he condemns the act, finds it hideous and unbelievable that he can carry it out, the more he moves toward an ability to do so, for he is separating himself from the person who is going to do the murdering. He can still have a high respect for himself to the extent that he is able to condemn the individual who will perpetrate such a heinous offense, for self-condemnation is not only cathartic, it is exonerating, proving that it is not he but some evil force within him that is the true offender against humanity.[5]

After the murders, Raskolnikov, while denying his guilt and searching for ways to escape apprehension, begins compulsively to talk about the crime, to leave hints of his culpability even among those who would otherwise be unsuspecting, all demonstrating that he is motivated on the unconscious level by a desire as well as a need to be caught as much as he is on a conscious level by the wish to escape from the arms of the law. His is a need to be punished, without which he is suffering greater punishment. Many of his actions are irrational and inexplicable, except as the very rational acts of someone manifesting such a punishment-demanding desire. The urge to confess is strong, but it will require articulation, and inasmuch as it must be accompanied by some hope that he will still be accepted, it can be made only to his two closest friends, Razumikhin and Sonya. By letting them know about his crime he will be suffering more, and hence expiating more, because he will suffer from the knowledge of the depths of the wounds he is inflicting on them.

Without a confession, Raskolnikov is an impostor, for those who love and accept him do so without knowing what he is because they do not know what he has done. Hence, for himself, there is no longer acceptance from anyone. Of the four meaningful people in his life, Razumikhin, Sonya, Dunya, and his mother, the acceptance or rejection of him upon learning the truth will provide the fullest test of whether humanity itself, embodied in its most loving and forgiving persons, can continue to count him in its ranks.

Confession is then both catharsis and torture, both relief and burden; or, placed in a slightly different perspective, the prospect of confessing is torture, the prospect of not confessing (which means not unburdening himself) is equal or greater torture. It can serve only as expiation if it is made to persons believing in him and unsuspecting of his secret and hence of his evil. It is perhaps the supreme punishment that he undergoes, and all else to follow is anticlimactic.

There are four related scenes dealing with self-disclosure, apprehension, confession, and denial that follow closely upon one another. The first is with Razumikhin, to whom he has by this time given many strong hints, who knows but will not permit himself to know. Razumikhin is in love with Dunya, and Raskolnikov takes solace in the knowledge that his sister and mother will not be alone, that they will have a

friend on whom to lean, and by confiding in this friend Raskolnikov is
reaching out to his family:

> Raskolnikov was waiting for him at the end of the corridor.
> "I knew you would come running after me," he said. "Go back to them,
> be with them . . . be with them tomorrow as well . . . and always. Per-
> haps . . . I will come . . . if I can. Good-bye!"
> And he walked away without offering his hand.
> "But where are you going? What do you mean? What is the matter with
> you? You can't do this sort of thing!" murmured Razumikhin, utterly at a
> loss.
> Raskolnikov stopped again.
> "Once for all, never ask me about anything. I cannot answer you . . .
> Don't come to see me. I may perhaps come here . . . Leave me, but . . .
> *don't leave them*. Do you understand?"
> It was dark in the corridor; they were standing near a lamp. For almost
> a minute they looked at one another in silence. Razumikhin remembered
> that minute all the rest of his life. With every moment Raskolnikov's intent
> and fiery glance pierced more powerfully into his mind and soul. Suddenly
> Razumikhin shuddered. Something strange had passed between them . . .
> some idea, something like a hint, something terrible and monstrous, sud-
> denly understood on both sides . . . Razumikhin grew as pale as a corpse.
> "Do you understand now?" said Raskolnikov abruptly, with painfully
> distorted features . . . "Go back, go to them," he added, turned away and
> hastily left the house . . . (P. 265)

This is a remarkable confession, because it is never made. From a
literary point of view, one can only admire the psychological depths
that are penetrated without explicit description, how and why and in
what manner recognition of an awful truth is resisted, the way in which
confession can be communicated without ever being stated, the startling
effect—"Razumikhin remembered that minute all the rest of his life"—
when the guards against disbelief are broken down and one is compelled to confront an inescapable reality. However, for Dostoevsky, the
punishment is insufficient, because the friends have parted without Raskolnikov ever having been forced to articulate the truth about himself
and the murders. There will have to be another confrontation, this time
with Sonya. It is a more difficult ordeal, because Raskolnikov's primary
concern is acceptance by Sonya, whereas with his friend Razumikhin it
was to receive assurance that he would protect the two women of the
family. His very last words to him are: "Go back, go to them."

From the encounter with Razumikhin, Raskolnikov goes directly to
Sonya. It is late when he enters her shabby room, and he is unexpected.
First they talk about Sonya and her stepmother and the children, of
illness and death. There is a moment's interlude. Suddenly he asks her if

she knew Lizaveta. She answers that she did know her and that Lizaveta was good, that she would see God. He now becomes irritable and drops his questioning about Lizaveta. This, of course, is what he has been doing since the killings, leaving hints, bringing up the names of the victims, compulsively and often in a self-incriminating way.

She takes out a Russian translation of the New Testament and he asks where she obtained it. From Lizaveta, he is told, and he implores her to search for the story of Lazarus. From the moment that Sonya reveals that she and Lizaveta had been friends, it is Lizaveta, not her pawnbroker sister, who is the central victim. Raskolnikov is doubly bound to Sonya, first by his need for her and his growing love, which can reach a goal only in the unburdening of a confession, and second by an understanding that he has killed a part of her in slaying her friend.

He has come to speak to her of something, he tells her, and she lifts her eyes to him in silence. They are both accursed, he and she, and so they belong together. He needs her, that is why he has come to her, he pleads, and she whispers that she does not understand.

"You will understand afterwards. Haven't you done the same? You too have stepped over the barrier . . . you were able to do it. You laid hands on yourself, you destroyed a life . . . *your own* (that makes no difference!)" (P. 278)

Sonya weeps hysterically and wrings her hands. Perhaps it is the last time that he will come to her, he says, but if he does come the next day, he will tell her who killed her friend Lizaveta. The statement startles her, and in innocence she asks whether he really knows who did it.

"I know, and I will tell you . . . You, and only you! I have chosen you. I shall not come to ask your forgiveness, I shall simply tell you. I chose you long ago to tell this thing to, when your father talked about you. I thought of it when Lizaveta was alive. Good-bye. Don't give me your hand. To-morrow!" (P. 279)

He still has not confessed, and although he has planted the idea as clearly in her mind as he had in Razumikhin's, she has not received the message. With an ever-increasing burden of anguish within, he is convinced that he must complete the confession. He reaches her lodging, filled with impotence and fear, and has second thoughts, asking himself whether he must tell her—not who killed the two women, but who killed Lizaveta. He feels incapable either of stopping himself from making the confession or of postponing what he believes has now become inevitable. Thus, in the worthy as in the unworthy, he is a man who relinquishes his freedom to inner demands.

When he announces that he has come to give her the name of the person who murdered her friend, she asks whether the murderer has been found. No, he replies, he has not been found. "Then how do you know about *it?*" she inquires (p. 346). He calls upon her to guess, explains that the murder of her friend had been accidental, only the first killing had been planned, and again he asks if she can guess, again she whispers that she cannot.

> "Look well."
> As soon as he had said this an old familiar sensation turned his heart to ice: he looked at her and suddenly in her face he seemed to see Lizaveta. He vividly recalled Lizaveta's expression as he advanced upon her with the axe and she retreated before him to the wall, with one hand stretched out and a childlike fear in her face, exactly like that of small children when they suddenly begin to be frightened, stare anxiously at the objects of their fear, shrink back and stretch out their little hands, ready to burst into tears. It was almost the same now with Sonya; just as helpless, just as frightened, she stared at him for some time and then, stretching out her left hand, lightly, almost imperceptibly, rested her fingers on his breast and slowly raised herself from the bed, shrinking farther and farther back, still with her eyes fixed on his face. Her fear suddenly communicated itself to him: the same terror showed in his face and he gazed at her with the same fixity and almost with the same *childish* smile.
> "Have you guessed?" he whispered at last.
> "Oh God!" burst in a terrible wail from her breast. (Pp. 346–347)

A few minutes later, he is imploring her not to torture him: this is his greatest punishment, his most agonizing suffering, to be compelled to bare himself before Sonya. And then she bursts out: "What have you done—what have you done to yourself?" (P. 347).

To *yourself*: the first victim of every crime is the criminal himself.

In her despair, she throws her arms around him, holds him tight: they are now two against the world. He tries to explain what had impelled him to do the things he had done, but his confusion overcomes him. If only he had killed because he was hungry, he might have found an excuse, he insists, and he tells her of his dream that by his act he was being transformed into a Napoleon. In the ensuing agonizing moments with her that follow the confession, he shifts the conversation toward the killing of the pawnbroker and brings forth his arsenal of justifications, but she answers him strongly, she is his voice of moral rectitude.

Then, the supreme search for a path away from responsibility. Yes, it was the wrong thing to do, but he had not done it:

"Did I murder the old woman? I killed myself, not that old creature! There and then I murdered myself at one blow, for ever! . . . But it was the devil who killed the old hag, not I. . . . That's enough, Sonya, enough, enough! Leave me alone!" he exclaimed in a sudden convulsion of anguish. "Leave me alone!" (P. 354)

She cannot leave him alone, any more than she can conspire to escape with him, or to help him escape. Give yourself up, she pleads, and then God will send you life again. "Accept suffering and achieve atonement through it—that is what you must do" (p. 355). When he rejects this counsel, and says that she is a child to make such a demand of him, she replies that he will destroy himself if he does not confess and suffer. "But to bear such torment!" she beseeches. "And for your whole life long! . . ." The torment is not the trial, exile to Siberia, imprisonment; the torment is to carry within oneself the knowledge of a sin that has not been expiated.

Before his confession to Sonya, Raskolnikov is with Porfiry Petrovich, the inspector assigned to the case, who in previous meetings had already given strong hints that he believes him guilty of the crimes. Porfiry plays with his prey, apologizes for having been unfair to him, begins to lead him down false paths, reassuring him that he is not a suspect. Raskolnikov is alarmed: "The idea that Porfiry might consider him innocent suddenly began to frighten him" (p. 380). They talk of false rumors, of how a guilty man behaves, describing the conduct of the murderer, so different from that of Raskolnikov himself. They go over the facts of the case, at least as much as they are known. There is the man Milkolka, being held as a prime suspect and who, in fact, has already confessed. Porfiry summarizes all of the attributes and actions of the murder, and suddenly, quietly, simply announces that Milkolka has had nothing to do with the crime: "There is no Milkolka in it!"

These last words, after all that had been said before, which had seemed like a recantation, were too unexpected a blow. Raskolnikov shuddered as though he had been stabbed.

"Then . . . who . . . was the murderer?" he could not help asking in a stifled voice. Porfiry Petrovich almost recoiled, as though he could not believe his own ears. "But it was *you*, Rodion Romanovich! You murdered them!" he went on, almost in a whisper, but his voice was full of conviction. (P. 385)

There is denial and protest, but they are indicative of Raskolnikov's ambivalence. Only surrender can lead to a new life. His ambivalence and his hope to escape are still with him when he meets Sonya for the one forthright confession that he makes. Both suicide and escape are rejected, because he hopes to live again, and neither road offers that possibility. When he enters the police station to make the announcement, he knows that Porfiry has little hard evidence against him: hence the surrender is made by choice. In the end, it is the choice he makes because he fears Sonya: she stands before him as an irrevocable sentence. If he is to live, there are two alternatives: the road that he has toyed with, denial and concealment and carrying the burden within, or hers, confession and expiation. But the first is not life because there is no rebirth.

Raskolnikov is a study in responsibility and the search to deny it. "In the bright realm of values," writes Jean-Paul Sartre, "we have no excuse behind us, nor justification before us. We are alone, with no excuses." The existentialist philosopher continues:

> That is the idea I shall try to convey when I say that man is condemned to be free. Condemned, because he did not create himself, yet, in other respects is free; because, once thrown into the world, he is responsible for everything he does. The existentialist does not believe in the power of passion. He will never agree that a sweeping passion is a ravaging torrent which fatally leads a man to certain acts and is therefore an excuse. He thinks that man is responsible for his passion.[6]

Sartre might well have been thinking of Raskolnikov when he wrote: "In one sense choice is possible, but what is not possible is not to choose. I can always choose, but I ought to know that if I do not choose, I am still choosing."[7]

The epilogue takes place in Siberia. Sonya follows Raskolnikov there, but he cannot be completely reconciled to the fact that he had chosen to commit evil and that the act committed was evil. Through the early years in prison, he never relinquishes entirely his justifications of the murder, at least of the pawnbroker (the other was accidental, although it illustrates that planned evil begets the unplanned). One day, after he has recovered from an illness in prison, he is alone with Sonya for a moment, the guard has turned away, and he weeps and throws his arms around her knees. They have only seven years left to wait for each other, and a new life will start, a new man will rise again.

Through love, humanity will be able to find the road to expiation. Through acceptance of responsibility, the past will be conquered because it will be admitted and recognized. There is no hopeless finality so long as there is a flicker of life.

NOTES

1. Richard Ellmann, *James Joyce* (New York: Oxford University Press, 1959), p. 499.

2. In Spanish the title is translated as *Crimen y Castigo*, the latter word closely related to the English *castigation* and closer to *chastisement* than to *punishment*.

3. In a February 1, 1977, private communication on the title, Robert L. Jackson, the American authority on Dostoevsky and professor of Slavic Languages and Literatures at Yale University, writes:

> The Russian word *nakazanie* basically can be used in *both senses* [punishment and chastisement]. *Nakaz* originally meant "orders," "instructions"; *nakazanie* is the penalty given out by somebody having the right or authority on one who has committed a crime or illegal act. The word can be used also in the sense of "retribution" and "chastisement." For example: *Kogo Bog ljubit', togo i nakazuet* (Whom God loves, He chastises). Or *Vsjakij prostypok nakazyvaetsja sovest'ju* (Every breach of manners—or fault—is punished by conscience). These two examples are taken from the 19th century dictionary by Dal'.

4. Fyodor Dostoevsky, *The Notebooks for Crime and Punishment*, ed. and trans. Edward Wasiolek (Chicago: University of Chicago Press, 1967), p. 172. (Originally published in Russian in Moscow and Leningrad in 1931.)

5. There is an analogous mechanism by which people dissociate their selves from their acts, through what Erving Goffman has called "role distance." However, in Goffman role distance is impression management; it is a manner by which people state that they are not the individuals (or types of individuals) that onlookers, the public, or the world at large apparently see. In Dostoevsky, as in Freud, the individual is stating this to himself: he is the one giving off the impression, the one receiving it, and the one about whom an impression is being communicated. See Erving Goffman, *Encounters* (Indianapolis: Bobbs-Merrill, 1961).

6. Jean-Paul Sartre, *The Philosophy of Existentialism* (New York: Philosophical Library, 1965), p. 41.

7. Ibid., p. 54.

3

MOLL FLANDERS
Happy Are the Days
of the Penitent

Moll Flanders was literature's first professional thief. More than that, *Moll Flanders* (the book, not the character) may mark a bifurcation in the development of the novel. The major trend in the new literary form, in England under Samuel Richardson and Henry Fielding, with deep roots on the continent in Rabelais and Cervantes, was the picaresque novel. But Daniel Defoe and a few others were primarily developing the episodic novel. The distinction is significant for the purpose of studying the confessions, true, fictional, and fictionalized truth, of the criminal. For in the picaresque, the central character is merely a mechanism through which the author is able to examine different places, people, happenings; thus, the work is deliberately constructed in a variety of settings and there is no continuity of plot or even of character. Coincidence, which was to be the bane of many writers for a century or more to follow, was not a concern, if only because persons once introduced could be abandoned and forgotten. In Defoe the very reverse is the case: the characters around whom the plots were built, the heroes or protagonists as they came to be called, were significant for themselves, for what they did, how they did it, where and with whom, to whom and with what consequences for themselves and others. It is within this context that one reads the view of James

---

All references without notes in this essay are to Daniel Defoe, *Moll Flanders*, Modern Library edition (New York: Random House, 1950).

Sutherland, that *Moll Flanders* might well be considered "our first sociological novel."[1]

In both forms of the novel, there is an emphasis on a world of exploration and discovery, for it is a literature that flourished in the era of colonialism and imperialism, when the French, British, Spanish, and Italians were discovering for the peoples of European culture the places that humanity had inhabited for millennia. With Defoe the emphasis is not on what the reader can learn of diverse places through the peregrinations of one person (the books cease to be travelogues—even *Robinson Crusoe* is not that), but on what the reader can learn through a fictional character who summarizes and symbolizes some aspect of the author's view of the world.

I do not mean to suggest that this was a sharp break, but rather a very gradual and almost imperceptible one, with Defoe taking one road and his best-remembered contemporaries the other. The reader is not entirely bereft of insights into Tom Jones's character because the author chose to use Tom's eyes not as mirrors of his soul but as spectacles, magnifying glasses, or telescopes to show us exactly what he saw. On the other side, certainly in *Moll Flanders* and to some extent in *Robinson Crusoe*, the world is not only observed but also interpreted through the eyes of the heroes. The emphasis here shifts, and what is of interest to us is that it shifts by the creation of two persons: the career or professional thief in *Moll* and the isolate despite himself in *Robinson*. They are one, or at least made out of the same cloth (there are similarities, as we shall see), and it should not surprise us that Daniel Defoe is the creator of both of these works, among many others of a more minor character including numerous essays. Moll Flanders and Robinson Crusoe are both alienated persons, to use the terminology of modern social science. They are both expressions of Defoe's view of humanity as people without bonds to one another, easily isolable, able to survive alone although with great loneliness, sorrow, and travail. And each has a strong economic motivation that is individualistic, rather than social, as befits the period in which they were created. Robinson's is a physical isolation. He is lost, abandoned by fate and by others, yet he survives; and overcome by the realization of his aloneness, his aim is both to find humanity again and to make his fortune in so doing. Moll's is a psychic alienation. She too is lost, because she has strayed from the ways of society and has loosened the social bonds that had held her to others, a process akin to what Emile Durkheim, Robert Merton, and other sociologists have called anomie. She is on her own, except for the few individuals who are her confederates in her criminal activities. She does not seek to find her way back to the world of others, but only to enjoy the fruits of her years of crime.

Both, further, see themselves as victims. In the tradition of persons who narrate their own stories, the protagonists in both novels are shown by Defoe to be persons who could lay claim to having little control over the distress to which they were reduced. Robinson is not a monastic recluse who has chosen solitude, he is forced into complete isolation: he finds himself in this fix, cries out in anguish against it, but does not resign himself to his fate. In an existential sense there was at first glance no choice; rather, something happened to him. He did not decide to be wrecked and to find himself alone. Only Defoe, as his creator, had a choice; he did not have to present this as his vision of humanity. But Robinson Crusoe does have a decision to make: he will swim rather than give up. Furthermore, he never ceases to plan and dream of his return to the arms of his fellow human beings, nor does he surrender to the immutable destiny that would have him live out the remainder of his life as an isolated person. There is always choice, as Georg Simmel suggested in his formal sociology and as the existentialists and particularly Sartre are constantly reminding us.

Moll Flanders also had choice. Defoe depicts her as someone infinitely capable of avoiding the responsibility for her actions by blaming her actions on people and circumstances not of her making. In that sense, and if for no other reason, this novel is an important milestone in the literary images of the criminal. In the first major work of literature in which the central character is a professional criminal and the central actions revolve around the crimes that are committed, Defoe presents a basic theme that is to plague criminology and criminal law. Should a person be made to take responsibility for his actions? Many of those in the positivist school of criminology, flourishing particularly in Italy in the latter part of the nineteenth century, were to answer this with a resounding negative: there is no free will, everything is determined, there are no miracles, all acts have antecedent causes, and hence one cannot be held personally responsible for one's actions. It is a world in which there are no choices, for the values that a person holds have been determined by previous history and forces beyond control, and the alleged or imputed choices that one makes on the basis of such values are shams and self-delusions. Punishment is never deserved, as Jeremy Bentham and the utilitarians in England, a century or more later, were to contend; it is only necessary. It must not be retributive or vengeful, but only a deterrent, a part of the totality that will result in determining the lives of others.

It is Defoe's contribution that, long before the raging of an endless debate on criminal responsibility and deterrence, he created in Moll Flanders a character who is able completely to exonerate herself for all wrongs that she has committed. She is the eternal blamer: things happen to her, people do her in, something takes hold of her. She is the constant victim, not so much of other people (there is a little of that, though she is much more the victimizer) but of fate, previous experiences, impulses that she cannot control, and of those who, against her own better judgment and sometimes even on her behalf, act improperly and unethically. Here is the epitome of escape from responsibility. In making such a presentation, Defoe presents an insight into the mind of the criminal that, if not penetrating, is an accurate mirror, reflecting without distortion the rationalizations that permit people to act in a way that, when the chips are down, they find indefensible. There is no golden rule for Moll Flanders; it is a world of all persons for themselves, as much as, and in a manner strikingly similar to, the world of Robinson Crusoe. The latter finds his man Friday and there is a mutual interdependence, almost a society of two persons; Moll Flanders has husbands, children, a mother, friends, accomplices, with whom she might have enjoyed emotionally gratifying experiences and relationships. But she does not need any of them except for what she can extract from them, and it is usually a monetary extraction, for she does not, or cannot, create with these others a microcosm of a social world in which such relationships can be fulfilling.

In this novel, there can be no guilt, atonement, expiation, or redemption, for in the mind of Moll there is never sin but only lawbreaking—at least never after the first acts of thievery and the temporary and short-lived remorse. Sin and crime are not at all interchangeable in her world, for the former involves an act against morality and conscience, the latter against a system of rules. Moll does wrong, but she seldom stops to contemplate this, for she is busy doing more wrongs or getting upset at others who do wrong to her. She breaks the law, but in her own mind she has no choice, given what has already befallen her. She leaves others as victims, but what can one expect, has she herself not been victimized? She is guilty, of that there is no doubt, but guilty without having guilt, without the penetrating suffering of one who believes that a sin has been committed and who is going to plead guilty and repent. Nor does she have the freedom that Sartre will find in Genet many years later: she is not freed from the fetters of social norms by having risen above them, but rather she has learned to avoid and evade these norms.

Moll Flanders can rationalize her acts, but in general she does not have to, for she is not on the verge of suffering or breakdown for having committed them. Rationalization is a choice forced on us when there is an internal belief that moral rules have been broken; it is not necessary when the transgressor is free of the most elementary moral restrictions. If Defoe was depicting the world as inhabited by amoral persons of whom the criminal is simply an example, as he seemed to be seeing it as a planet of isolated persons of whom the castaway was almost perfect as an example, then his was a bitter and pessimistic view of humanity. If, like Edwin Sutherland and others who were to come later, he was painting only the career thief or other career criminals and was telling us that by their failure to face moral issues they permit themselves to continue in their profession (one hesitates to call it a chosen profession), then his portrait may bear a greater resemblance to the world of reality, particularly two or almost three centuries after he wrote, than do many studies in the social sciences today.

What marks Moll Flanders's life through the years of thievery is the failure of Defoe, save for a fleeting moment, to have her experience any remorse and expiation. There are few regrets, except at being apprehended, and the only wish that things had been different (other than that one or two of the less successful efforts at thievery had come off better) arises from the failure in some instances to get away scot free. Perhaps one is attributing too much to Defoe to read into this omission some deliberate design.

Moll Flanders is an early achievement in the history of the novel, and like the picaresque efforts, it is a story of adventure, not an analysis of the mind. This is the age-old problem of interpreting art and literature, of the validity of finding therein what the author may not have intended—a dispute that assumed new dimensions when literary and other critics discovered the unconscious.

In the end, it does not matter whether Defoe omitted the self-flagellation because he was not as penetrating as Dostoevsky or because he was more accurate in portraying the world of common and ordinary thieves (in which case we would say that Raskolnikov is an extraordinary criminal). What concerns us is that the absence of guilt or even the acknowledgment of it is a significant commission by omission; it is a forceful message, that there are criminals so concerned with the acts they are planning and performing, with avoiding arrest, reaping benefits, planning anew, finding collaborators, choosing victims, learning techniques, that they become immersed in crime as a career and a way of life and give little thought to sin and harm. There is no inner suffering, and the failure to depict it, intended or not, is itself a depiction of its failure to be present. It is a savage and shallow world that Defoe offers, without social communion among its inhabitants, without moral reflexes linking and binding persons to one another, a world of exploitation and manipulation. If it is to be extended beyond criminality and into everyday interaction, it is as strong a message of doom, as biting an indictment of humanity, as the work of his contemporary, the dean of St. Patrick's, who also wrote, in *Gulliver's Travels*, an amusing and harmless adventure story for children.

Scruples are well-nigh absent in the life of Moll, at least after her first downfall when as an innocent virgin she has permitted herself to be seduced by a man she loved with longing and fidelity, only to become the mistress he seeks to discard, trying (ultimately with success, but to her everlasting chagrin) to turn her over to his younger brother as wife. This is the beginning of her road down, and note that it is another who does something to her; she loves, she is innocent, she believes in the other and is faithful to him, only to be betrayed. It is always the evil other person who is responsible.

There is one moment when scruples do overcome Moll, and interestingly, a reflection of the times, it is in the area of sexuality. She is in one of her many marriages and affairs, and travels with her husband to meet his mother in America. In Virginia, her mother-in-law confides to Moll her deepest and longest-held secret: that she, the mother-in-law, is an exconvict. Once apprehended, she had been sent to Newgate, where she would have been hanged had it not been for the fact that she was with child. In prison (she places the exact time), she gave birth to a daughter, who was taken from her; the mother was then transported to Virginia, an exile to a desolate colony. Moll listens with increasing interest, fear, suspicion, and horror, for she herself had been born at just that time, to a prisoner in Newgate, and the evidence becomes insurmountable. She is talking to her mother, who is also her mother-in-law. She is married to her own brother (in fact, and to be more exact, her half-brother, a difference that does not in the least mitigate the sense of horror that this arouses in her).

Incest is a favorite theme in the fiction of crime, sin, deviance, and guilt. It was made prominent by Freud's interest in Sophocles, but beyond this, it occurs (in literature at least) with remarkable frequency.[2] For it offers the novelist an opportunity to create an act that is entered into with the innocence of ignorance, and yet, once discovered, that brings forth the strongest sense of guilt. For the first time, Moll repents with depth and over a sustained period for what she has done; thus, her repentance is aroused only by an act the nature of which she did not know and could not understand at the time that she committed it, and which she would not have performed had she understood its ramifications and import. It is only the sinner *malgré soi* who repents, not the deliberate transgressor! Pledged to secrecy by her mother, Moll Flanders simply ceases to be wife (at least sexually) to the man to whom she is wedded. Eventually, she leaves him to return to England, but only after exacting from her mother a pledge that, when the old lady writes her will, she will be sure to leave a good portion to the departing daughter. They part, the loving mother (who does fulfill her promise), the adoring daughter (who comes back, some years later, to collect her due). It is at this point that one may well pose the question: Does Defoe, by creating these sets of circumstances with sinister perfection, wish to exculpate Moll, if not to expiate her?

Through more than half of the novel, the acts of Moll are mainly those of deception and her victims primarily men in hot pursuit of her, although in the first major episode she is victimized by one of them. She has her fortunes and her misfortunes, but she is not yet a professional thief; in fact, other than men whom she seeks to exploit and who have the same designs upon her, a matter of reciprocity that does not hold later for the victims of her thievery, she is living the life of a lawful woman. But misfortunes accumulate, and her first entry into the world of crime is carefully delineated, a combination of poverty, temptation, and the devil:

> I lived two years in this dismal condition, wasting that little I had, weeping continually over my dismal circumstances, and, as it were, only bleeding to death, without the least hope or prospect of help from God or man; and now I had cried so long, and so often, that tears were, as I might say, exhausted, and I began to be desperate, for I grew apace. (P. 180)

And then, a few lines later, preparing the reader for the worst:

> Oh let none read this part without seriously reflecting on the circumstances of a desolate state, and how they would grapple with mere want of friends and want of bread. . . . (P. 180)

at which point she quotes what she calls the wise man's prayer, "Give me not poverty, lest I steal." And continues:

> A time of distress is a time of dreadful temptation, and all the strength to resist is taken away; poverty presses, the soul is made desperate by distress, and what can be done? (P. 180)

The foundation for the criminal career has been laid; now all it requires is the proper set of circumstances. Crime, as many modern criminologists have put it, is often unplanned, is situational, and requires the opportunity to commit it, as much as the lack of opportunity to reach monetary and other desired goals through normative means. Moll wanders around town, crime still the furthest thought from her mind, until she sees a little bundle wrapped in white cloth on a stool in an apothecary shop, while the two persons in the shop are standing, their backs to the door, busily engaged in talking to each other. Nobody else is in the shop.

This was the bait; and the devil, who I said laid the snare, as readily prompted me as if he had spoke, for I remember, and shall never forget it, 'twas like a voice spoken to me over my shoulder, "Take the bundle; be quick; do it this moment." It was no sooner said but I stepped into the shop. . . . (P. 181)

and she is off with the bundle. But let us not be unfair to Moll, nor oversimplify Defoe: "It is impossible to express the horror of my soul all the while I did it." (Impossible? Well, it must have been extremely difficult, for neither Moll nor Defoe tries.) Lord, what am I now, a thief? she asks herself, and fears that she will end up in Newgate. What torment! Why, it lasts some three or four days.

Soon there is another opportunity, this time to steal a little necklace of gold beads from the neck of a child. Moll Flanders thus continues in the life of crime on which she has so recently embarked, although at the same time expressing, in the most self-congratulatory manner, the inherent goodness within her, that manifests itself in the reiteration of her wish to live as a penitent. With starvation ahead, however, and crime so simple to accomplish and so temptingly beckoning, she is trapped. She suffers with "an evil counsellor within" who is "continually prompting me to relieve myself by the worst means" (p. 183). She goes out and meets a little girl, leads her to a dark alley, and with fingers that are becoming more adept in their skills, relieves the child of her gold beads:

Here, I say, the devil put me upon killing the child in the dark alley, that it might not cry, but the very thought frighted me so that I was ready to drop down; but I turned the child about and bade it go back again, for that was not its way home. (P. 184)

Poverty is making the heart heavy. Nevertheless, this last affair

left no great concern upon me, for as I did the poor child no harm, I only said to myself, I had given the parents a just reproof for their negligence in leaving the poor little lamb to come home by itself, and it would teach them to take care of it another time. (P. 184)

The compassion is touching. The best interests of the child, plus the twelve or fourteen pounds that the beads will fetch, constitute full justification, so that if there is any movement toward remorse, it quickly dies. First, the internal compulsion, that evil counsellor within, and then the lack of harm and in fact the social good that the act brings about, and all this in the midst of poverty and starvation which beckon as the only alternatives to crime. These hardly comprise a milieu in which repentance will thrive.

However, I did the child no harm; I did not so much as fright it, for I had a great many tender thoughts about me yet, and did nothing but what, as I may say, mere necessity drove me to. (P. 184)

Moll Flanders has embarked at this point on a career, and for Defoe she is more than the professional criminal, she is an entrepreneur. It is the age of individualism, and in an ironic twist of the Protestant ethic and the homilies of Benjamin Franklin, Moll Flanders embodies the spirit of Calvinism.[3] Each person for himself. Moll had done little more than go into business for herself. In the final judgment based on the ethic of success, the only failure is to get caught or to be unsuccessful in the new calling. She wavers little. Occasionally she stops to count her booty, she organizes, shares, plans, but as a successful business-woman she is unlikely to retire from a lucrative occupation. It is not a business that one can sell; and although one may obtain partners, as in fact she does, she can hardly hope to build up an enterprise of size and standing. So that she is faced with the choice between starvation and destitution and the voluntary relinquishment of a good thing.

Some episodes do not come off too well for the narrator. A comrade is caught and in fact executed, being an old offender. What happens to this comrade serves as a terrible example, and again Moll Flanders is the perfect embodiment of the infinite capability of the human mind to rationalize one's wrongdoings and thus evade responsibility. Just as something within, that evil counsellor, and something without, the prospect of ever-worsening starvation, are responsible for the acts, it is not a sense of moral righteousness but the example of the executed comrade that almost brings her back to a life of propriety. In an existential sense, she never confronts the need to decide between right and wrong, because Moll is adept at evading the question. Nor are we to take Defoe to task for the inadequacies of his characters: he is depicting the mind of the criminal, or of some criminals, with remarkable accuracy. Moll Flanders combines the lower-class need to exist, at all costs and by any means possible, in a society in which the opportunities are few and the oppression indisputable with the upward mobility drive of the petty bourgeois. In her view, like that of Karl Marx some years later, the exploitation, cheating, chicanery, large- and small-scale larceny of the upperworld serves as example, excuse, and justification, making her enterprise no different in its moral implications from the flourishing businesses of the wealthy.[4] She could think of herself as a female Robin Hood, if only she donated her loot to the poor, and if only she could concentrate exclusively on victimizing the rich.[5]

Her business is like others, except for the possibility that she may get caught. This is the underworld's analogue to mercantile decline and bankruptcy. If one is apprehended, the authorities are merciless; the world has little time or sympathy for its failures. For those not frightened into toeing the line by the punishment after a first offense and a conviction, and who return to their incorrigible ways, there is death. Even as this fate awaits Moll Flanders, she offers only the most meager evidence of repentance.

Apprehended in what has become a daily routine of crime, she is committed to Newgate, where she is thrown into company with others like herself. It turns her "first stupid and senseless, then brutish and thoughtless, and at last raving mad as any of them were." That is all she needs to become acclimated to the place, which will be a temporary abode at best:

> I had a weight of guilt upon me enough to sink any creature who had the least power of reflection left, and had any sense upon them of the happiness of this life, or the misery of another; then I had at first remorse indeed, but no repentance; I had now neither remorse nor repentance. I had a crime charged on me, the punishment of which was death by our law; the proof so evident, that there was no room for me so much as to plead not guilty. I had the name of an old offender, so that I had nothing to expect but death in a few weeks' time, neither had I myself any thoughts of escaping; and yet a certain strange lethargy of soul possessed me. I had no trouble, no apprehensions, no sorrow about me, the first surprise was gone; I was, I may well say, I know not how; my senses, my reason nay my conscience, were all asleep; my course of wickedness, whoredom, adultery, incest, lying, theft; and, in a word, everything but murder and treason had been my practice from the age of eighteen, or thereabouts, to threescore; and now I was engulfed in the misery of punishment, and had an infamous death just at the door, and yet I had no sense of my condition, no thought of heaven or hell at least, that went any farther than a bare flying touch, like the stitch of pain that gives a hint and goes off. I neither had a heart to ask God's mercy, nor indeed to think of it. And in this, I think, I have given a brief description of the completest misery on earth. (Pp. 265–266)

It is a strange misery that she describes as the completest on earth. It is a wretchedness that consists in her inability not only to ask forgiveness, but even to feel a need, a want, to do so. It is not because her heart is so heavy with the ill deeds of the past that her God will not listen. She does not even think of this as she awaits death. So what is this, the completest misery? It is the inability to feel a sense of misery. Hardened like stone, petrified not by fear but by lack of feeling, it is the brutishness that has overcome her that she laments. "Sometimes," writes Elizabeth Drew, "we feel that the only thing Moll really dislikes about the life of a thief is that it brings her into contact with such a low class of person!"[6]

The book is presented as memoirs, and supposedly was written years after the events being described. Moll will survive, as novelists so neatly arrange that their protagonists do. So what she may be saying, as she writes these words down long after, is that at the moment when she faced death in Newgate, she was completely unrepentant; and thinking back on this in her golden years of retirement, when she is a well-to-do senior citizen, she beholds the lack of repentance as the epitome of misery. The book itself, then, in its presentation as a confessional, is the ultimate repentance, but hardly one that will serve as a warning to those still being tempted. Moll Flanders is the happiest of all penitents.[7]

She does not go to her death. Have no fear. With her many comrades, lovers, husbands, confederates, someone will turn up to save her. One of her many exhusbands is brought into prison, a highwayman for whose downfall she feels utter and complete responsibility (interesting self-flagellation for the eternal blamer, who can never believe that she is the one who has done herself in). Recalling that she had been the occasion for the original mischief of this former spouse, she is determined to save him. She in fact succeeds and she too is spared. Both are transported to Virginia, where she learns, to no great sorrow, that her mother is dead. She reveals to her son in America (children are born, die, disappear, sometimes reappear in this book, with the author apparently little aware of any need for continuity in his story, occasionally returning someone who has dropped out of sight for the convenience of the plot, but more frequently forgetting an individual no longer required) that she is his mother, presents him with a watch without informing him that it is stolen, and lays claim to the fortune that her mother has indeed left for her. She is concerned about the fate of her half-brother to whom she had been married, the son's father, but it is a negative feeling: more ill one could not wish on anyone.

Now in good straits and in a good life she lives for some time, but yearns to return to England, where she can reside in comfort and be a woman of respectability. She and one of the exhusbands, with whom she has formed a new and more permanent alliance, count their money and their belongings. They have arrived: they are in excellent circumstances, almost upper class, aristocrats except for lack of pedigree. She can go back and forth to her son while almost incidentally collecting an annual income from a plantation, and on one of these trips she learns, and confesses that it is not disagreeable news, that the incestuously married brother-husband is dead. It is on this note that the book ends:

> It must be observed that when the old wretch my brother (husband) was dead, I then freely gave my husband an account of all that affair, and of this cousin, as I had called him before, being my own son by that mistaken

unhappy match. He was perfectly easy in the account, and told me he should have been as easy if the old man, as we called him, had been alive. "For," said he, "it was no fault of yours, nor of his; it was a mistake impossible to be prevented." He only reproached him with desiring me to conceal it, and to live with him as a wife, after I knew that he was my brother; that, he said, was a vile part. Thus all these difficulties were made easy, and we lived together with the greatest kindness and comfort imaginable. We are now grown old; I am come back to England, being almost seventy years of age, my husband sixty-eight, having performed more than the limited terms of my transportation; and now, notwithstanding all the fatigues and all the miseries we have both gone through, we are both of us in good heart and health. My husband remained there some time after me to settle our affairs, and at first I had intended to go back to him, but at his desire altered that resolution, and he is come over to England also, where we resolve to spend the remainder of our years in sincere penitence for the wicked lives we have lived. (Pp. 327–328)

Thus they spend the remainder of their lives, suffering in comfort and repenting in the moments that can be spared between the days and nights of joy. Is Defoe laughing at the reader in this last sentence, is he chuckling with Moll Flanders as she emphasizes the sincerity of the penitence and the wickedness of her life?

Long titles were very much the style, and books came to be known by their abbreviated titles, but the lengthier sometimes revealed an author's intent and interpretation. Thus, Defoe called his novel:

The Fortunes and Misfortunes of the Famous Moll Flanders Who was Born in Newgate, and during a Life of Three-score Years, besides her Childhood, was Twelve Years a Whore, five Times a Wife (whereof once to her own Brother), Twelve Years a Thief, Eight Years a Transported Felon in Virginia, at last grew Rich, liv'd Honest, and dy'd a Penitent. Written from her own Memorandums . . . [Ellipses at end of original title]

It is not clear from the enigmatic title whether the seventy years that were hers were in addition to her childhood, or included it. At any rate, she is elderly when she writes the memoirs, and after the years of thievery and exile, it appears that there is little time left to become a penitent. As for the other information in the title, yes, she was born in Newgate, hardly a good beginning. She was a thief and transported felon, but there is little sign that for twelve years she was a prostitute, or for any time at all, unless Defoe is using the word "whore" to describe the sexually available woman. She was far from promiscuous, merely "living in sin" on occasion, as an old saying would have it. The marriages described in the title are accurate, if the reader can count them as the tale runs along at a fast pace, but Defoe as well as Moll seemed to be more concerned with the incestuous relationship than with any of the deliberate harms that she committed. But at last she grows rich. Of course, her businesses are a success, and even her transportation for crime led to her obtaining an inheritance from a mother who had herself been a transported felon. Finally, she lives in honesty, as Defoe announces in his title, and like twentieth-century millionaires who retire from organized crime as philanthropists and pillars of the community, she can well afford to do the same on the ill-begotten earnings, savings, and inheritance, not to mention the royalties on her memoirs.

But died a penitent? We do not know for sure, because it is a book of memoirs, and she might have lived on, but Defoe offers no evidence except his title and her bald statement. To the extent that this is a believable story and a credible character, one must see that her capacity for repentance was ephemeral at most, to be conjured up when she found it useful, and not to endure long enough to interfere with the life of a professional thief. Penitence implies acceptance of responsibility, and her long confessional is one self-exculpation after another. Penitence means more than I did it, it means that I accept the burden for having done it, and nowhere is this evident.

After a lifetime in crime, Moll retires to write her memoirs, a confessional in which she does not reveal her true name. It is her last task. "The book serves many of Moll's needs," writes Everett Zimmerman. "Confession purges her of guilt. Also, she can savor her past as she severs herself from it; her obvious pleasure in her criminal triumphs is excused by the morals that she now draws."[8]

Hardly a description of someone suffering in her years of penitence. Nor would anything else be expected. "When Moll disintegrates," this same critic Zimmerman states, speaking of her collapse in Newgate as she awaits what will almost certainly be the terrible noose around her neck, "Defoe fails to define any moral world that exists outside her consciousness. Like Moll, he presumably accepts a Christian view of repentance and redemption. . . . Inner chaos must be suppressed by some order, however arbitrary. Defoe is driven to assert out of fear, not out of belief. In this, too, he resembles his creature."[9]

In his studies of the English novel, Edward Wagenknecht states:

> Moll Flanders *rightly* sees herself as more sinned against than sinning, the inevitable product of a social system which makes starvation the only alternative to prostitution for an unprotected girl and then smugly casts stones at her because she chooses to live. [My emphasis][10]

It is a widely held view, not only of Moll but of all criminals, although interestingly enough Wagenknecht, in exculpating the heroine, points to prostitution, not thievery, as the only alternative to starvation. Ian Watt notes some apparent discrepancies in the character of Moll, and then states that these "might reasonably be resolved by assuming that Moll Flanders is naturally warm-hearted but that circumstances often *force* her to play a lone hand."[11] (My emphasis)

Naturally warm-hearted? Perhaps so, although there is only her own self-serving account by which to judge, and it all adds up to a warm-heartedness that cooled with rapidity after her seduction and abandonment by her first lover. But circumstances forcing her? This is Moll's own complaint, everything evil she did was beyond her control, and hence she is free from responsibility.

But Mark Schorer does not exclude choice and hence does not exculpate. He writes of the "small choice that Moll could have made between disreputable and reputable employment."[12] The cards were indeed stacked against her, but not to the exclusion of choice.

One of the problems that critics have with Moll Flanders is that she is so much like Defoe, but it need not be a problem for criminologists or other social scientists. For to the extent that there is similarity, her method of looking at her criminal career, or excusing it while it is occurring and pretending repentance at a later date, is Defoe's own outlook on himself, the individual, and the society. Along this line, Ian Watt writes that Moll Flanders is similar to her author in several respects:

> She seems fundamentally untouched by her criminal background, and, on the contrary, displays many of the attitudes of a virtuous and public-minded citizen. . . . Moll Flanders obviously places criminals into two classes: most of them are vicious reprobates who richly deserve their fate; but she and a few of her friends are essentially virtuous and deserving people who have been unfortunate.[13]

Why, then, the penitence? The answer is simple: there is none. Her condemnation of other criminals, those unlike herself, is understandable as the rationalizations of a woman of middle-class ideology who insists on clinging to her own vision of herself as a morally righteous person and at the same time not relinquishing the pleasures of her immorally obtained goods. "Indeed," states Watt, "her most positive qualities are the same as Crusoe's, a restless, amoral and strenuous individualism."[14]

It is the individualism of alienation, to use the terminology of modern social science. Zimmerman writes of the episodes of *Moll Flanders* that they "are carefully, even rigidly, organized to illustrate the loosening of Moll's moral inhibitions and social ties."[15] And further: "But Moll cannot even be part of the community of thieves; her fellow criminals soon become her gravest danger. Repeatedly she is saved because others are not. She gets the 'joyful News' that an accomplice is hanged."[16]

Not to be lost in the discussion of this book is the fact that the central character is a woman. In eighteenth-century thought, the concept of the female as an individual capable of discerning moral judgments, able to pursue an independent life, was foreign to a male-dominated society. The description of Moll's behavior may in part be ascribed to the psychology of women prevalent at the time of Defoe. In criticizing Defoe, rather than Moll, of duplicity, we should not fail to recognize that he tried to imbue his fictive character with traits assumed to be characteristic of women. It was no more a matter of chance that his dissolute criminal was a woman than that his castaway was a man.

But he does not exonerate males. In a manner that was later to be followed by Tolstoi in *Resurrection,* it was a male who first led the good woman astray, and males who subsequently deepened Moll's immersion into a criminal way of life. Nor is it irrelevant that in the eighteenth century the common criminal was thought of as an inferior being, much like savages, slaves, and women. Dominant social thinkers, largely of upper-class origin and training, could only view the plight and fate of the under classes as the "natural order of things," and those who violated that order, the criminals, as even lowlier.

Moll evades guilt, evades a chastisement of self, by ascribing her criminality—while barely acknowledging it—to a servility of will. That is the essence of her rationalization: her vulnerability to forces beyond her control. Nineteenth-century criminologists, while conceding that the criminal carried out his actions for reasons determined by forces outside his will, nevertheless imposed upon him a responsibility; it was social responsibility, but not personal responsibility.

For Defoe's novel, the moral issues appear to focus on an important dimension of crime and humanity. From Defoe's perspective, society as such never seeks the salvation of the individual, but demands only justice. Execution, incapacitation, banishment, all of which were prevalent at the time, could not save souls, they could only remove them. Perhaps Defoe is suggesting through the callousness of Moll, certainly not through her putative penitence, that it was not reasonable to invoke a moral justification for punishment that might be called retributive. Paralyzing the poor and deprived people with fear and terror was the main source of social order, not the widespread belief that each person had an obligation and a stake in complying with the law.

As the memoirs of a penitent old woman who has retired from her life of crime, written as befits memoirs in the first person, the book permits the true author, through his prefatory remarks, to place a distance between himself and the criminal. The evil deeds, the countless excuses, the rationalizations, the blaming on others, the failure to see the moral issues, the lack of loyalty to accomplices, many husbands, and even more children: this is the chronicle of Moll. But all that Defoe can say in his preface is that she died repentant. This has led some critics, who find the repentance less than convincing, to interpret the entire work as irony, but there is little evidence that that was Defoe's intention. For the social scientist it is the nature of the repentance itself, the conditions under which it manifests itself, whether it is real or fake, that loom important.

"What confirmation of her repentance can there be?" asks Zimmerman. "She is confined to her solipsistic prison. Her search for the 'satisfaction' and 'comfort' of repentance is successful only after she is sentenced to death: she finally believes in her repentance when it can no longer serve an earthly purpose."[17] But she does not die, and Zimmerman here notes that "repentance in the face of death does not solve the problem of living. Moll must learn again to deal with her world; having no principles, she again parodies respectability."[18]

But perhaps the preface is written with tongue in cheek, claims Elizabeth Drew. If so, this does not come through to many critics, and could not to Defoe's readers. There is not a wicked action in any part of the book, Defoe states in his preface, and notes further that Moll is "first and last rendered unhappy and unfortunate" (p. xxi), all of which for Drew is such obvious nonsense that "it is difficult not to believe that the whole preface is intended ironically."[19]

Many people have taken her penitence seriously, the supposed irony of the author notwithstanding. James Sutherland writes of Defoe that "he was willing to meet his heroine half way, but she had to be punished, and she had to show an awareness of her immorality and at least some signs of repentance." He warns us not to forget that "it is the penitent Moll, writing in her old age, who is telling us her story."[20]

Perhaps, in the end, we will rest with the judgment of Mark Schorer, that "the book is not the true chronicle of a disreputable female, but the true allegory of an impoverished soul—the author's; not an anatomy of the criminal class, but of the middle class striving for security."[21]

And it is Schorer who summarizes in words that are of interest to the criminologist:

> Moll Flanders comes to us professing that its purpose is to warn us not only against a life of crime but against the cost of crime. We cannot for very many pages take that profession seriously, for it is apparent all too soon that nothing in the conduct of the narrative indicates that virtue is either more necessary or more enjoyable than vice. At the end we discover

that Moll turns virtuous only after a life of vice has enabled her to do so with security.[22]

Therein, curiously enough, may lie the value of the document. It is an "own story" of a professional thief, a convicted felon, a liar and deceiver, who has had no problem in coming to peace with herself. Nor did the felons who inhabit the true stories of criminologists, unlike those found on the couches and in the chronicles of Freud and his disciples.[23] The professional thieves were not sick with guilt or neuroses; they knew when they had a good thing going, and they knew when to stand up and tell the world that they were sorry. The time to do so was when they were living in retirement, off the fat of the land and the fruits of their labor, or when they could use a few extra dollars from a publisher's contract. Whether so intended or not, Defoe has penetrated into the mind of the career criminal who cannot accept the onus for any action, who has justifications and excuses for everything, who is adept at the game of blaming, and who, hence, her own protestations (or his) to the contrary, cannot die a penitent because she could not live a penitent. What is there to repent, after all, when all that has happened is the fault of poverty, seducers, devils that put you up to things, and uncontrollable and hateful urges that come from the evil counsellor within, one knows not whence?

NOTES

1. James Sutherland, *Daniel Defoe: A Critical Study* (Cambridge, Mass.: Harvard University Press, 1971), p. 179.

2. The literature on incest is so vast that it is worthy of an entire study in itself. Like Sophocles, many writers deal with involuntary incest, between persons who do not know that they are related. In *Mourning Becomes Electra* Eugene O'Neill depicts a father-daughter relationship, but it never becomes explicitly sexual; then, in *Desire Under the Elms,* a son-stepmother relationship (the son and stepmother are of about the same age). There is a combined sexual-amorous interaction between brother and sister (not without the knowledge of each) in a pre-Hitler German novel, Günter Birkenfeld's *A Room in Berlin,* and then in a curious work of Thomas Mann, *The Holy Sinner.* In this last book, the brother-mate is banished, and the child set adrift; and like Oedipus, he returns to woo his mother. Thus Mann combines the innocent incest (of the Moll Flanders type) with the deliberately chosen brother-sister affair. And Mann returns to brother-sister incest in a famous short story, "The Blood of the Walsungs." But these are just a few titles in a literature that may be greater than the infrequency of the event warrants.

3. This suggestion, and the comparison between Moll Flanders and Robinson Crusoe in their entrepreneurial ambitions, comes from Ian Watt, *The Rise*

of the Novel: Studies in Defoe, Richardson and Fielding (Berkeley: University of California Press, 1964).

4. Note what Karl Marx in *Theories of Surplus Value* has written along this line:

> A philosopher produces ideas, a poet poems, a clergyman sermons, a professor compendia, and so on. A criminal produces crime. . . . The criminal produces not only crimes but also criminal law. . . . The whole of the police and of criminal justice, constables, judges, hangmen, juries, etc. While crime takes a part of the superfluous population off the labor market and thus reduces competition among the laborers—up to a certain point preventing wages from falling below the minimum—the struggle against crime absorbs another part of this population. Thus, the criminal comes in as one of those natural "counterweights" which bring about a correct balance and open up a whole perspective of "useful" occupations.

5. Another interesting area for study is a comparison of female criminals in belles lettres with those in the criminological literature. In Shakespeare we can go to Gertrude and to Lady Macbeth, but the novel has given us more females as adulteresses, like Madame Bovary and Hester Prynne, than career criminals in the sense that Moll Flanders earned that label. There is a rich and growing criminological literature on this theme, including the works of Cesare Lombroso, Sheldon and Eleanor Glueck, and the recent and controversial book by Freda Adler, *Sisters in Crime: The Rise of the New Female Criminal* (New York: McGraw-Hill, 1975).

6. Elizabeth Drew, *The Novel: A Modern Guide to Fifteen English Masterpieces* (New York: Norton, 1963), p. 32.

7. "It is only fair to notice," writes an anonymous author in the famed eleventh edition (1910) of the *Encyclopaedia Britannica* (Vol. VII, p. 929), "that while the latter [Moll Flanders], according to Defoe's more usual practice, is allowed to repent and end happily, Roxana is brought to complete misery; Defoe's morality, therefore, required more repulsiveness in one case than in the other."

8. Everett Zimmerman, *Defoe and the Novel* (Berkeley: University of California Press, 1975), pp. 84–85.

9. Ibid., p. 106.

10. Edward Wagenknecht, *Cavalcade of the English Novel* (New York: Henry Holt, 1943), pp. 39–40.

11. Watt, *Rise of the Novel*, p. 105.

12. Mark Schorer, Introduction to Modern Library edition, p. xv.

13. Watt, *Rise of the Novel*, pp. 113–114.

14. Ibid., p. 114.

15. Zimmerman, *Defoe and the Novel*, p. 85.

16. Ibid., p. 87.

17. Ibid., p. 90.

18. Ibid., p. 91.

19. Drew, *The Novel*, p. 30.

20. Sutherland, *Daniel Defoe*, pp. 183–184.
21. Schorer, Introduction, pp. xiii–xiv.
22. Ibid., pp. xii–xiii.
23. In the literature of criminology, the concept of crime as a profession, occupation, career, vocation, and, to a slighter degree, avocation is often called the "own story," not always an accurate title for it has frequently been told by another. It is linked with the name of Edwin Sutherland, dean of American criminologists and towering figure in criminological thought for at least a generation. Sutherland's concept of the career criminal was given impetus by the title perhaps even more than by the contents of one of his best-known works (if it can be called his, for it was largely an autobiography of another, for which he wrote an introduction and copious and important notes). The book is *The Professional Thief* (Chicago: University of Chicago Press, 1937). Among works in the same genre that preceded it perhaps the most important was Hutchins Hapgood, *The Autobiography of a Thief* (New York: Fox, Duffield, 1903). Later there came an account of bad-check writers by Bruce Jackson, *A Thief's Primer* (New York: Macmillan, 1969), safe crackers by Bill Chambliss, *Box Man: A Professional Thief's Journey* (New York: Harper & Row, 1972), and Carl B. Klockars, *The Professional Fence* (New York: Free Press, 1974). A very influential work that preceded Sutherland's was Clifford R. Shaw, *The Jack-Roller* (Chicago: University of Chicago Press, 1930); it may have been the first to use the term "own story," which came to describe this entire genre of literature.

In all of this, Sutherland's influence cannot be gainsaid. Not that there was any dearth of autobiographies of murderers, thieves, men of the underworld, political criminals, prostitutes, and many others. But what Sutherland and some of his followers, and his predecessors as well, did was to give professional guidance to the unfolding story, describing, annotating, accepting, and analyzing the world as it appears through the eyes of the criminal.

In a sense, then, they were writing novels, although not fiction; novels because these were stories about people, with character, a little plot, plenty of episodes, some development, and occasionally a bit of suspense. But everything was true. This does not mean that they were *romans à clef,* and they were certainly not presented as such, for there is no interest on the part of the reader in identifying who a character with a fictional name is supposed to be in actual life. Identities were concealed for protection. The proper name of a person or place was changed, or some small modification of another sort was introduced that would in no way impeach the integrity or credibility of the story (for it was a story), but that would leave people who had cooperated with the criminologists with protection from being apprehended or becoming inadvertent informers.

These works are in part derived from the social-psychological effort to see the world from the vantage point of the other, and they constitute a synthesis with psychological and particularly psychoanalytic reports. The sociologists were largely filling in the social environment in which the crime was seeded and flourished, and even more were describing the *modus operandi* of the criminal, so much so that at times these became "how to" books—it is to be hoped they were not read by impressionable students seeking to gain learning and knowledge for purposes unintended by authors and professors. At the same time, the psychoanalysts were complementing such works with studies of the minds and motivations, particularly the tensions between the consciousness and the unconsciousness, of the individuals.

But both types of work had a history, a forerunner largely ignored by the sociologists but less so by the psychoanalysts: literature in its pure form, belles lettres, and not in the social scientific or just scientific manner in which that term is used. True as their stories were—Sutherland on the one hand, Freud on the other—they were writing novels in a literary tradition that can be traced, as Freud indeed did, to the mythologies of primitive peoples, the earliest theological documents, the dramas of the classic Hellenic era, and then flowering again after the Middle Ages and during the latter part of the Renaissance in a form that came to be called *le roman,* the novel, the story of romance. In this historical development, Moll Flanders certainly plays a major role: before Sutherland came on the scene, and antedating Freud by some two centuries, she was a Chic Conwell without annotations, an Isabella or an Anna without Freud's hermeneutics.

4

JEAN VALJEAN
For Stealing
a Loaf of Bread

Jean Valjean and Raskolnikov are probably the two best-known images of the criminal in the history of literature. Their creators were contemporaries: each a major figure in a mid-nineteenth-century movement in his own country, each at times an exile, and each surrounded by others with whom he formed, if not at the time then at least historically, an enriching oeuvre that brought the novel forward by great strides. Both were social critics who used the medium of the novel to plumb the depths of human degradation.

Nevertheless, the two characters are a study in contrast. For what marks Raskolnikov is the inescapable responsibility that he must bear for what befalls him, and what delineates Jean Valjean is the essential innocence of the man. If he were innocent only in the sense of having been falsely accused, his would be a different tale, and probably one with far less significance for us.[1] Jean Valjean does indeed commit the act that sends him to the galleys and that is the beginning of his downfall. Hugo's supreme indictment of society—for this *is* an indictment of society (he was a forerunner of Zola and other novelists who saw themselves as social critics)—lies in the nature of the act which his

---

All quotations and references in this essay are from Victor Hugo, *Les Misérables,* trans. Lascelles Wraxall (New York: Heritage Press, 1939). There have been numerous other translations. This is one of the few novels that I would advise the serious reader to read in an abridged version.

hero has perpetrated and for which he is imprisoned. Literally, Jean Valjean is guilty of stealing a loaf of bread.

It would appear that such an act would ordinarily evoke only sympathy and hence require no further mitigation in order for an author to exculpate his "criminal" and to paint him as the purest and most saintly of all beings (one is almost compelled to use quotation marks around *criminal,* so that Hugo's relentless efforts to remind the reader of Valjean's goodness are rendered with integrity). To this end, the taking of the loaf of bread is an almost perfect transgression, and the breaking of the law is justified or at least extenuated by the forces of hunger, poverty, and the execrable social conditions that followed the counterrevolution in France. But Hugo goes even further than this, and in so doing betrays a weakness not only in the literary work but in the social criticism: it is not for himself and his own stomach that Jean Valjean commits a theft. He does not even so much as expect to taste a morsel of the stolen bread. It is for his sister's children, young, fatherless, and hungry, that he becomes a thief. So two factors are here at work, and as they follow the reader throughout the five volumes that make up this novel, they detract from each other rather than act symbiotically to strengthen the motifs: there is the social indictment, and there is the criminal as saint.

Les Misérables is one of the few titles that have come into the English language in the original, without being translated. One hardly requires a knowledge of French to understand it: quite obviously, it means the miserable ones, the sufferers, perhaps best captured in the phrase from "The Internationale" (not yet written when Hugo created Jean Valjean) that was used by Fanon: *the wretched of the earth.* The criminals, the persons in the galleys, the convicts and even more the exconvicts, not only are these the wretched of the earth, but among them are also found many of the saints. Not all, for there are several exceptions in this world of good people and evil. Save for some minor delicts performed in a moment of wavering, Jean Valjean is depicted as a man who cannot be surpassed in his strength of character, his essential goodness, altruism, sacrifice, in short, his saintliness.

Starting with the criminal as victim, Hugo continues with the criminal (or more accurately the exconvict) as the embodiment of virtue. He is the penitent incarnate, but he has never done wrong and has nothing for which to repent. Over and over he redeems himself. Without a blemish on his past, however, the redemption is ill-placed. What emerges, from the viewpoint of the social critic, and in contrast with other great literary images of the transgressor, is a series of unintended ambiguities, with messages not as clearly drawn as are even the one-dimensional characters who inhabit the novel.

In his studies of French literature, the distinguished critic Lytton Strachey wrote of *Les Misérables:*

> In that enormous work, Hugo attempted to construct a prose epic of modern life; but the attempt was not successful. Its rhetorical cast of style, its ceaseless and glaring melodrama, its childish presentments of human character, its endless digressions and—running through all this—its evidences of immense and disordered power, make the book perhaps the most magnificent failure—the most "wild enormity" ever produced by a man of genius.[2]

But it is not only for the literary critic that it is a "magnificent failure"—it is for the social scientist as well, seeking insights into the minds of the hunted and their hunters. However, it is in the ambition of the author, in his "immense and disordered power," that many themes come forward in sharp relief.

The first of these is conversion through kindness. Out of prison after a term of nineteen years, a bitter, hardened, and prematurely aged man, Jean Valjean is rebuffed wherever he goes to seek lodging, although he has money in hand. He carries the *carte d'identité* of an exconvict that he must show before he can rent a room: it is the mark of Cain, and all the world shuns him. He stumbles into the home of a bishop, a man living with his sister and a housekeeper, and there he, a child of God, is made welcome. He is seated at a dining table on which are placed two silver candlesticks and six silver plates, and he is given a bed (he, an exconvict, has not slept in one for nineteen years, he tells the bishop). During the night or early hours of the morning, he awakens and hurries quietly out of the house, but not before stealing the silver plates. Soon he is apprehended (but not because of any alarm by the bishop or anyone from his household) and brought back to the house to be identified as a thief. He is about to be arrested and will surely be sent back to the galleys, this time for life. The bishop smiles and tells the constables that he has indeed made a gift to the man of the allegedly stolen silver, and turning to the frightened, surprised, and cowering Jean, reminds him of the candlesticks which had also been given him as gifts, but which he had mistakenly left behind.

This might be the logical scene for a flash of light, an almost miraculous Biblical-style conversion much like that of Saul of Tarsus. But such a sudden conversion would interfere with the intricately planned plot: it is essential that this exconvict actually commit another crime, and not one from which he will be exonerated by the benefactor whom he has victimized. The story that ensues is one of changes of identity, pursuit, concealment of a past, apprehension, and escape, all made necessary because he is wanted for a new offense.

If Jean Valjean is going to be painted as pure and saintly, and he is, the theft from the bishop and a subsequent incident with a little boy from whom he takes a coin are the blemishes—these, and not the stealing of the loaf of bread. Through the many years to follow until the last moments of his life, and through the countless pages and the episodes, coincidences, acts of strength, heroism, and sacrifice, there will be nothing but these two acts that are short of Christlike purity. What is Hugo telling us, then, when so good a person as his hero steals first from the bishop and then from the boy Gervais? That it is prison that brings out all that is worst in man, that turns the potentially best into the most wretched, that leaves one bitter and angry, seeing all humanity, even a man of God and a child, as enemy. Oscar Wilde, out of his own tragic experiences, was to say the same some three decades later in "The Ballad of Reading Gaol": "It is only what is good in Man/That wastes and withers there."

In the message of Hugo, it is kindness, in its most extreme and unexpected form, that alone can bring reform or even instant rehabilitation, not through guilt or expiation but through rebirth and resurrection. Love, Victor Hugo is telling us: love, and the wretched mass of humanity will be redeemed. Man is essentially good, more than good, he is pure and heavenly, he needs only to be shown the other cheek and he will embrace and kiss it, not rebuff and repel it. Jean Valjean is the embodiment of this, but how universal, or how convincing even in his own instance, is a matter of dispute.

Despite the bishop and the silver plates, Valjean has not yet perceived the flash of light that will cause his instant redemption. The last flicker of bitterness has not been extinguished when, wandering, he meets a boy whom he cheats out of a coin. Realizing the enormity of his cruelty when the boy Gervais, having lost his two-franc piece, goes off crying, Valjean runs after the lad. He searches for the boy, cries out his name, trying to overtake him to return the money. Unable to find him, he gives the coin to a curé, and with it more coins as well, money for the poor, and sees himself as a galley-slave, a robber, a convict, a total wretch. In complete despair, he seats himself and begins to sob. He was dazzled when confronted with the virtue and kindness of the bishop and then, only a short time thereafter, there was the encounter with Gervais. We are given a glimpse of a man in the process of conversion, of the forces of good and evil struggling within him, each seeking victory over the other, the classic theological battle for possession of a man's soul between the devil and God's angels:

One thing which he did not suspect is certain, however, that he was no longer the same man: all was changed in him, and it was no longer in his power to get rid of the fact that the bishop had spoken to him and taken his hand. While in this mental condition he met little Gervais, and robbed him of his two francs. Why did he so; assuredly he could not explain it. Was it a final and, as it were, supreme effort of the evil thought he had brought from the bagne, a remainder of impulse, a result of what is called in statics "acquired momentum"? It was so, and was perhaps also even less than that. Let us say it simply, it was not he who robbed, it was not the man, but the brute beast that through habit and instinct stupidly placed its foot on the coin, while the intellect was struggling with such novel and extraordinary sensations. When the intellect woke again and saw this brutish action, Jean Valjean recoiled with agony and uttered a cry of horror. It was a curious phenomenon, and one only possible in the situation he was in, that, in robbing the boy of that money, he committed a deed of which he was no longer capable. (Vol. 1, pp. 108–109)

It is a profound passage, and worthy of considerable attention. Hugo has caught his character in the very act of change, at the moment of duality when he is traveling from evil to good and both are present as adversary forces. He is neither one person nor the other, neither the convict hardened, gloomy, and bitter against the world nor the redeemed man who has had a vision of the beauty that resides in the good and is beckoned to it. He is neither in the pure sense, because he remains both, as anyone at a moment of change must be. For Hugo, he is one of the two persons (or personalities) in his impulses, instincts, and habits, and he is the other in the intellect which is freeing him (or seeking to do so) from the nineteen years of the constant formation of an evil self. When his intellect sees what his habits have brought him to, he recoils, he denies that it is he (the eternal evasion of responsibility, it was not I, it was something in me, something that drove me), he repents and seeks to undo the act. It is Schopenhauer's eternal enmity between the worlds of will and idea, and it is a forerunner of Freud and the struggle between the unconscious and the intellect. In Valjean, the idea and the intellect will triumph.

Now he must run, run endlessly, for as a second offender, he will, if seized, be returned to the galleys for life. Hugo implies some condemnation of the judicial and penal systems, their harshness and cruelty, but essentially they are tangential to his story and even occasionally interfere with it. The galleys are not filled with Jean Valjeans but with men whose delicts are far more serious than the theft of a loaf of bread, and there is not a great deal that Hugo has to say about these men or their conditions of servitude. Here and there a word suggests suffering and cruelty, but Hugo seems to have known little about the actual conditions prevailing for prisoners, and his book falls short as an important indictment. If it is not an example of successful rehabilitation, for there was no evil in the protagonist but only in the society that condemned him, it nevertheless contradicts the strongly believed tenet that prison itself corrupts. All that is necessary for Jean Valjean to make his way in society is to conceal that he is an exconvict and, as the event with the child makes him, a fugitive as well.

Jean Valjean does not find the child and, unable to make restitution except in the symbolic sense of giving to charity, he runs away. We next encounter him as a highly successful manufacturer who has become mayor of his town and probably the most benevolent capitalist that the French bourgeoisie had ever known. Only his name is changed, and how he has accumulated the capital to reach the pinnacle of success is of little interest and is something on which Hugo spends no time. It is one of the ironies of the work that at this moment he is departing from his condemnation of the bourgeois society and instead gives us an example of the fluidity of the social classes, the upward-mobile channels on which this protagonist travels. Employers and capitalists can be good; their capitalist class interests need not (and in the instance of Valjean do not) interfere with their beneficence. The entire town prospers, and M. Madeleine, as he is now known, is more beloved than any, and deservedly so.

There are intricate subplots in the five volumes that make up the book, but they do not seem to be afterthoughts, as one finds in *Moll Flanders* or in the works of the feuilletonists. A character may be put aside, but he will be met again, in a passage without which the work cannot go forward to its logical conclusion. All of this makes for the long arm of coincidence reaching out with greater length than even an avid admirer of nineteenth-century literature is ready to accept. One such character M. Fauchelevent (later, when he requires a new identity, Jean Valjean will pose as this man's brother, and for a long time will be known by his surname) is crushed under a horse and wagon, and is being pushed into the soft earth. He is only minutes away from certain death. Standing by at the scene are many people, including Jean Valjean (under the identity of M. Madeleine, of course), and singlehandedly, for strength of body is a virtue that he possesses and that symbolizes strength of will and character as well as determination, he lifts the entire wagon and the horse and frees the grateful man. Gratitude is not forgotten, as Valjean is to learn much later.

Watching this scene is an inspector, the antagonist and enemy, the incarnation of devotion to unflagging duty as much as Valjean is of goodness. If Valjean is the saint, Javert is the petty French bureaucrat. The inspector has never before seen such a demonstration of physical strength. He marvels at it, and then, in a flash, recalls that yes, once before, he saw a man of similar herculean physical prowess. It was in the galleys, and the man's name was Jean Valjean. He suspects that the merchant is an exfelon, now wanted for another crime, and resolves to discover the truth. If M. Madeleine is only the pseudonym of the former galley slave now wanted for a second offense (the theft of the coin), he will be arrested.[3] To verify the true identity, Hugo creates a setting where the downfall of the merchant, his unmasking, is the result of a great act of heroism and sacrifice rather than the work of a rather clever detective. In fact, it is a two-part act of heroism: the first is the demonstration of strength in saving a life, thus creating a suspicion where none existed before; the second takes place in a courtroom.

Javert comes to believe that the link he has made in his mind between M. Madeleine and Valjean is false, and he comes to the mayor to offer his apologies, telling him of the mistaken notions that he has harbored. How does he know that he has been mistaken? Because the real Jean Valjean has just been seized and identified despite his denial, and will soon go on trial as a second offender. Javert asks to be forgiven for the evil thoughts that he has had about M. Madeleine. The scenario is unavoidable: Valjean walks dramatically into the courtroom to save an innocent man from being victimized by an error of the courts. A short time later he is seized, as he knows he must be, and walks off with stoicism and internal gratification to what might well be the rest of his life in the galleys.

There are numerous subplots that are unraveled, the major one involving Fantine and her illegitimate daughter, Cosette. Fantine asks the Thénardiers to take care of Cosette and sends a monthly allowance. The Thénardiers are the evil side of Hugo's coin, in the simplistic world of good and bad people. They starve and maltreat the little girl, constantly demand more money from her mother, use the money to clothe and feed their own daughters, and make a slave out of the child who is all of about five years of age. Nothing in the literature of fairy tales is drawn with sharper or simpler lines: Cinderella and the evil stepmother is a story of one happy and compassionate family in comparison.

Fantine has lost her job in M. Madeleine's factory (through no act of which he has knowledge, it hardly need be added). She struggles and starves herself to send money to the Thénardiers for the care of Cosette; she even has two teeth extracted so that they can be sold. She is dying when Valjean learns of her plight and comes to her rescue. It is too late to save her life, but at least he can fetch the little girl for the dying mother to see, and can pledge that he will care for her. Not so easily accomplished, for the Thénardiers become suspicious that the mother has fallen into money, and in their greed they make greater and greater demands before they are ready to give up the child. Valjean attempts to obtain Cosette so that the dying mother can see her before she expires, but in vain. However, before her death, Fantine signs and turns over to Valjean a precious piece of paper that will enable him legally to make claim to the little girl. At this point, Javert leads Valjean to the galleys, a fate to which the latter has exposed himself lest an innocent person be punished.

Escape is still another act of heroism. This time it is to save a sailor from certain death; and after rescuing the man, Valjean falls or drops into the sea and is swallowed up between ships. His obituary appears in the paper, where it is seen by Javert. But Javert and others have not counted on superhuman strength, and Valjean will rise from the sea as he has risen before; will return to the scene where, before his rearrest, he has hidden his money as well as the letter from Fantine; and will manage, not without great effort, to obtain the little girl from the clutches of the Thénardiers.

The themes are now repeated: sacrifice, goodness, and strength on one side, evil on the other. Had Valjean been a different person, or had there been others from the galleys like him, he might have symbolized what Hugo seems haltingly to be suggesting at times: the criminals are the saints, and their jailers are the sinners. But Thénardier and many others are evil criminals, and aside from Valjean himself there are none that epitomize goodness. Only one man has risen, and in the end he is one who had never fallen.

Kindness, rather than forgiveness, is the key to the rescue of Valjean from the world of bitterness, for there is nothing to forgive; if anything, it is he who must forgive the world for the treatment that he has suffered. Kindness is remembered, and it is repaid. M. Fauchelevant, the man whose life Valjean saved, is given an opportunity to harbor him when he and Cosette become fugitives. Javert, the archenemy, the one person whose death would give Valjean an opportunity to breathe easier in the knowledge that he will no longer be so relentlessly pursued, is about to be executed during the insurrectionary days of 1832—and Valjean saves him. But duty calls, and the incorruptible French officer of the law cannot waver; he must rearrest even the man who has but recently saved him from certain death. Unable to bring himself to make that arrest, the inspector commits suicide, a failure, a man who has dishonored those who have put faith in him.

André Maurois has written glowingly of this work. He praises its literary qualities, the excellent prose, the historical frescoes (the description of the Battle of Waterloo, and a more detailed one of the barricades on the streets of Paris in 1832). It is, however, a narrow view, for while Les Misérables has these virtues, Maurois ignores its faults—how ill-drawn the characters are, how absurd the plot, how unsubtle the unweaving of the story, as one compares it with the works of the giants of the French novel who came just before Hugo and during his lifetime: Balzac, Stendhal, Gautier, and particularly Flaubert. But then Maurois finds in it great moral qualities, the painful quest of heroism and sanctity. "Doubtless in this quest almost all men fail; but it is precisely because of their personal failures that they like to meet, in a noble book, heroes who, better than they themselves, have conquered their basest passions."[4] It is an interesting evaluation, and heroism and sanctity are indeed here present—frequently, self-lessly, passionately, unmistakably. No reader can fail to discern the message. There is satisfaction in finding in another these qualities that one cannot attain oneself, but a reader must wish that there really were base passions in Valjean, and that he had actually conquered them and not merely overcome a momentary bitterness that arose because of the inhuman treatment he was accorded following the theft of the single loaf. If only there had been sin, there might have been redemption. Valjean never rises from the basest passions because he had never descended. The thefts of the bishop's silver plates and of the child's two-franc coin, which he sought to return: these and the loaf of bread are all that we have against him; for these he must spend a lifetime of expiation.

Yet there is expiation. I am not sure, as Maurois contends, that this is the sort of book that gives one "greater confidence in life and in himself." Maurois writes of *Les Misérables* that it speaks more to man of "his liberty than of his slavery."[5] Yes and no, but it depends largely upon the willingness of the reader to suspend confidence in the univer-sality of almost all other characters and utilize the hero as symbol of humanity. For Valjean does have liberty to rise, despite the pursuit by Javert, innumerable social pressures, and the social conditions that caused hunger and virtual thralldom.

Victor Hugo evidently gave great importance to the loaf of bread, and *Les Misérables* has left a legacy to the language of irony, that in the world of unequals he who steals a million dollars becomes a prime minister or an industrial tycoon while he who steals a loaf of bread ends up in prison. Jean Valjean spent nineteen years as a galley slave for his theft, about which Hugo writes in one of the passages in which he departs from his role of novelist and becomes essayist, social commen-tator, or historian:

> This is the second time that, during his essays on the penal question and condemnation by the law, the author of this book has come across a loaf as the starting-point of the disaster of a destiny. Claude Gueux stole a loaf, and so did Jean Valjean, and English statistics prove that in London four robberies out of five have hunger as their immediate cause. (Vol. 1, p. 85)

Here is Hugo as the critic of society: it is a world populated by prisoners of starvation, and it drives good men to crime. It is a world of cruelty and injustice, and it determines the destiny of men such as Jean Valjean. His, the author's and the hero's, is a cry from the depths of despair. Yet the message of Hugo actually is that all that is good in man cannot be destroyed by the prison air (Wilde notwithstanding), not *all* that is good, and not in *all* good men. It can only be driven beneath the surface as one hardens in the struggle for survival.

If this is a story, or even the story, of man rising to heights from the lowest depths, it is also a story of man seeking to escape from a past, to conceal it, to find a manner of starting life anew without pursuit from others and without the cloak that must be worn if one's stigma is to remain invisible.[6] In the first instance, one almost wishes that the rise to heights were to places somewhat less lofty. Maurois is understating when he draws attention to the inability of the reader to fulfill a similar quest for heroism and sanctity. The fact is that Jean Valjean is just too good to be true, and this becomes literal for the reader who cannot immerse himself only in the man as symbol and wants to see him as a living person and to be confronted with greater verisimilitude with his fate.

Hugo's artistry, nonetheless, with all its shortcomings, does present us with an individual who captures our interests; very much as in the old-fashioned cinemas that were continued from week to week, as the hero or heroine hung from the cliffs while the enemy was in hot pursuit, so we read breathlessly and applaud inwardly as Jean Valjean narrowly escapes doom. This is particularly telling in a scene in which he is seeking to escape from his pursuers by being carried out in a coffin that is supposed to contain the body of a dead woman. The plan of his friend Fauchelevent is to pretend to be taking the coffin off for burial, only to allow the hero to escape when they are alone. But the plan begins to go awry. Valjean is almost buried alive, and one can well imagine that someone might die of fright during an episode of this sort. But the reader knows that the protagonist will not meet his death by being buried alive, if only because there are hundreds of pages to go and they cannot be filled without him, and also because there are too many threads left hanging and Hugo had to wind things up in an orderly manner. However, there is a height of excitement as one wonders how Valjean will get out of this fix; those who watched Houdini must have felt something akin to the fear and the expectations, the certainty that all will be well in the end, that overcome the reader of this passage.[7]

What all this adds up to is that Jean Valjean is a sympathetic symbol, but more than a symbol. At times he does emerge as a meaningful personality, even if no one else in the novel has the same good fortune. As symbol, however, Valjean is never at the lowest depths, never has been, and here Hugo fails us. Essentially, Valjean was not converted, especially since his first crime had not been anything other than an act of sacrifice, of altruism, of goodness. Raskolnikov did murder, he killed the pawnbroker and her sister with a hatchet; he planned the murder, and his was an act of baseness. And, as we shall see, Lord Jim did abandon ship, as no captain or mate ever should, leaving aboard the sinking vessel the men under his command in contravention of his vows and the moral order of the sea. Moll Flanders stole and stole and stole. But what Hugo has given us is more of a condemnation of society (as his aside on the subject of four out of five English crimes would indicate), and for that reason his novel cannot rank as a study in human redemption. There was really no crime, or so little of one. Valjean had never been a Raskolnikov; Raskolnikov could never have been canonized by Dostoevsky.

Like Lord Jim, Jean Valjean is seeking to escape from a past, but there the analogy ends. Lord Jim never wants to be faced by anyone who has learned of his misdeed because it was an act of infamy; it is really from himself that he wishes to find refuge. An impossible task: there are no worlds without mirrors. So while Lord Jim's secret protects him from inner persecution, Valjean's secret must guard him from the outer world, for two reasons: first, because the world will demand a penalty if he is apprehended and his identity disclosed; and second, because the world will never cease condemning an exconvict. There are only *les condamnés* in the world of Hugo; there are none who can be called *les anciens condamnés,* although they might be called *les anciens prisonniers.* Man, once condemned, is forever condemned; he may be released from the bagnes, the galleys, the walls and bars, but he remains always in prison once he has been there. There is no Christian world that forgives anyone, not even this man for whom there is nothing to forgive. One pays forever, and at best can live only by concealment. The biography is there and cannot be rewritten, but it does not have to be told, or it can be falsified (and the two are essentially one). In this sense, if there is a message that Hugo wants us to learn from the life of Jean Valjean, the book is still very much alive. Ask any exconvict, in France or the United States and probably most other countries of the world, and they will tell you that the world of Jean Valjean remains almost unchanged among us. If these exconvicts were to be sanctified, it would give them as little solace as it did Hugo's central figure, for where is the audience that would believe the glorifiers, or perform the canonization rites, except perhaps a century and a half after their death?

The departures that the author takes from his novel in order to offer social commentary often have only tangential reference to the plots and subplots of the book, but they are significant in themselves. Hugo is, as it were, reminding himself that he is writing a story of the wretched, not of one individual, and even if the two clash it does not concern him. "All the crimes of the man begin with the vagabondage of the lad," he states (Vol. III, p. 10), although it was hardly true of Jean Valjean and there is little evidence of it in the criminal underworld elements with whom Valjean comes into contact at certain points in his adventures. And there is a longer, bitter, less than subtle passage on what is done to the youth of Paris (there is some material here of more than passing interest to the historian of juvenile delinquency):

> In the reign of Louis XIV, to go no further back, the king wished, rightly enough, to create a fleet. The idea was good, but let us look at the means. No fleet is possible, unless you have by the side of the sailing vessels, which are the playthings of the winds, vessels which can be sent wherever may be necessary, or be used as tugs, impelled by oars or steam; and in those days galleys were to the navy what steam-vessels now are. Hence galleys were needed, but galleys are only moved through the galley-slave, and hence the latter must be procured. Colbert ordered the provincial intendants and parliaments to produce as many convicts as they could, and the magistrates displayed great complaisance in the matter. A man kept on his hat when a procession passed; that was a Hugenot attitude, and he was sent to the galleys. A boy was met in the street; provided that he was fifteen years of age, and had no place to sleep in, he was sent to the galleys. It was a great reign—a great age.
>
> In the reign of Louis XV, children disappeared in Paris; the police carried them off, and no one knew for what mysterious employment. Monstrous conjectures were whispered as to the king's purple baths. It sometimes happened that when boys ran short, the exempts seized such as had parents, and the parents, in their despair, attacked the exempts. In such a case parliament interfered and hanged—whom? the exempts? no— the fathers. (Vol. III, pp. 10–11)

It is not merely a passage of this type, where exposition interrupts the novel, but similar themes implicit throughout the work that inspire Arthur Waldhorn to write of the book: "With overpowering pathos the French poor of the post-Napoleonic era are portrayed in this vast panorama."[8] And David Evans: "No writer of the century rendered greater service than did Hugo to the cause of social justice."[9] And a biographer, Paul Berret: "He was under all forms of government the advocate of all the disinherited, all the unfortunate, all the oppressed, nations or individuals; a boundless pity was the unfailing impetus of the social reforms he proposed or supported."[10]

Certainly there are few lives in which the ledger would add up so overwhelmingly to the credit side by some bookkeeper at the gates of heaven as does that of Jean Valjean. He adopts Cosette (not legally), protects her, educates her at a convent, loves her as a guardian, father, and grandfather, and is prepared to see her take leave of him for the man who seeks to marry her. The man is Marius, and here at times Hugo is romanticizing not only the poor but the rebel. Marius has renounced his riches (this occurs before he meets Cosette), because he has renounced his grandfather who was responsible for his separation from his father, and whose political affiliation is anathema to him. He has embraced poverty and work: "The poor young man has to work for his bread, and when he has eaten has only reverie left him" (Vol. III, p. 120). How lovely! And again:

> When his work is ended, he returns to ineffable ecstasy, to contemplation and joy; he lives with his feet in affliction, in obstacles, on the pavement, in the brambles, or at times in the mud, but his head is in the light. He is firm, serene, gentle, peaceful, attentive, serious, satisfied with a little, and benevolent, and he blesses God for having given him two riches which rich men often want—labor which makes him free, and thought that renders him worthy. (Vol. III, p. 120)

This glorification of the proletariat, which was to come into vogue in the early years after the Russian Revolution and which fits in so neatly, although it came from another direction, with the ideology of oppressors and bourgeoisie, is soon abandoned by the youthful Marius. He makes his peace with his grandfather and the latter's wealth, and when he finally marries Cosette, there is a complete reversal: a glorification of luxuries and the softness of life, of the styles and qualities of living as befit two members of the bourgeois-aristocratic classes. Until that day, Marius, like Jean Valjean (whom he does not know except that he has seen him with the girl Cosette), was a saint among sinners. He starves but shares. He gives more than he keeps. He has thirty francs between himself and destitution, but when a neighbor is about to be evicted for lack of twenty francs in rent, he pays the landlady not twenty francs but twenty-five, and admonishes her not to tell the tenants where the money came from. He is not merely on the side of the angels, he is one of them. And what can be said of poverty? It has turned him to virtue, although fortunately for himself and Cosette, they will be able to retain their lofty ideals without being eternally bound to the poverty that had made it possible for him to embrace them. That is the best of two possible worlds, indeed!

A passage that refers to the underworld, the literal criminal underworld though it might be equally applicable to the world of fear of exposure in which Jean Valjean lives, summarizes perhaps as well as any in this novel what Hugo has to say about crime:

The social evil is darkness; humanity is identity, for all men are of the same clay, and in this nether world, at least, there is no difference in predestination; we are the same shadow before, the same flesh during, and the same ashes afterward; but ignorance, mixed with the human paste, blackens it, and this incurable blackness enters man and becomes Evil there. (Vol. III, p. 160)

It is more than Jean Valjean that Hugo is discussing when he writes that the social evil is darkness, it is humanity. If only humanity could accept the brotherhood of man, know that we come from nothing and will return to nothing, that the short time between need not be wretched for the millions of poor, *les misérables,* then we could live in harmony and love on earth. Have no illusions: we are not predestined, Calvinism notwithstanding, to eternal damnation or endless bliss. We all have the same future, the darkness of the grave, and if we could lift ourselves from the ignorance that does not accept this, we could bring light into a world of somber shadows. This is Hugo's hope for salvation, but it is a meager hope, and in the end only Jean Valjean finds this salvation, only one unusual soul among millions of ordinary folk. Our sins are greater than thefts of loaves of bread for the hungry and the young, and we will not be able to fulfill en masse the hopes that Hugo expresses so eloquently in this passage.

It is no wonder that Tolstoi considered Hugo's novel, according to Evans, "the finest work of art in the nineteenth century," many opinions to the contrary notwithstanding.[11] If this is an exaggeration born of admiration for sentiments and philosophy so lofty that the faults can be overlooked, one cannot but admit and admire the deep influence that the book must have had on Tolstoi himself. Particularly in the last thirty or forty pages of *Resurrection,* Tolstoi, through his central character, Nekhludov, who was born a prince but had witnessed the degradation of prisoners, expresses his outrage against injustice, against man's inhumanity to man. He writes, in words that might have come out of *Les Misérables,* that the condemners are as guilty as the condemned. Yet, there are differences in the outlooks of the two authors. At the end of his travail, writes Tolstoi, Nekhludov

saw quite clearly that the only sure means of salvation from the terrible wrong which man has to endure is for every man to acknowledge himself a sinner before God and therefore unfitted to punish or reform other men. It had become clear to him now that the terrible evil which he had witnessed in jails and halting places and the calm self-assurance of those who were responsible for it resulted from the attempt by men to perform the impossible. Evil themselves, they presumed to correct evil. Vicious men undertook to reform other vicious men and expected to accomplish this by mechanical means. The only result was that needy and greedy men, having made a profession of so-called punishment and correction, became utterly corrupt themselves, and unceasingly corrupted those whom they tormented.[12]

The author of *Les Misérables* never quite states that all men are sinners, as does Tolstoi, or even that all have the potential for becoming sinners, as Dostoevsky so forcefully although implicitly argues. Instead Hugo believes that in kindness and forgiveness humanity can overcome the forces of evil. Here Tolstoi and Hugo become as one. Writes Tolstoi, again from *Resurrection:*

> For many centuries people considered as criminals have been executed— but have they become extinct? No; far from diminishing, their numbers have been increased by the addition of those who have been demoralized by punishments, and also of those other criminals—judges, prosecutors, magistrates, and jailers, who judge and punish men. Now Nekhludov understood that society and order still existed in general, not thanks to these legalized criminals, who judge and punish other men, but because in spite of their depraving influence men still love and pity one another.[13]

Wherein, then, can one find the answer? It is in the message, Tolstoi teaches, that Christ gave to Peter:

> . . . to forgive everything, everyone, to forgive unceasingly, never to grow weary in forgiving. There are no men living who do not need forgiveness, and therefore there are no men living fit to correct or punish others.[14]

At best, and in the end, Jean Valjean seeks the ultimate forgiveness: he must end the masquerade and make known, at least to Marius and Cosette, his true identity. What is he? A perennial fugitive, an exconvict, a man who has served in the galleys. The stigma of the past follows, and he feels sullied and unworthy of these two young people. He relinquishes the girl whom he has cared for over the years, he renounces the right and the possibility of a continued relationship with her by making his confession to Marius. It is a voluntary act. On countless occasions he has come near being trapped, not by Marius but by Javert, Thénardier, and others, and has always escaped. Now, of his own volition, he feels himself the impostor who must tell these two about his past. It is not what he has done but the fact that he has been branded, forever labeled an exconvict and a fugitive, that is the burden of his life.

In making his confession, is he seeking only to obtain the catharsis that both Catholicism and the free association introduced by Freud have proved so liberating? Or is he desiring, in the subterranean world of his own unconscious, to be embraced by Marius, who will insist that the past is irrelevant? Hugo here seems to have forgotten that Marius is only recently a revolutionist, has just come from the barricades; his bourgeoisification, or rebourgeoisification, is rapid and complete. Marius shrinks back when he hears the confession. And he does not accept the man, whom he has known as Fauchelevent, who is now revealed as Jean Valjean.

The story cannot end there. At the last moment, Marius will embrace our hero, he will unite himself and Cosette with Jean Valjean and, on the latter's deathbed, give him a moment of supreme happiness such as he has seldom encountered during the years of life. But Marius does not rise to the moral stature of Jean Valjean, and if one is critical of Hugo for oversanctifying his hero, one can be even more so for his treatment of Marius. For, in the final act of accepting Cosette's benefactor, Marius does so for essentially the wrong reasons.[15] He learns that this is the man who has saved him, by carrying him through the sewers of Paris, as he bled and was dying on the day of the battle of the barricades. He had known of the rescue, but knew nothing of the identity of his rescuer. Now, to his joy, he discovers that it was Valjean. It is but one of the countless coincidences that make up the book, but this time it is not the improbable unfolding of the plot that concerns us but the moral failure Hugo depicts: the failure to offer forgiveness, to extend the hand of morality for its own sake. Marius is repaying a debt, and there is no philanthropy in such an act. His is a symbolic gesture not of virtue but of gratitude. One can find some mitigation if one searches. It can be said, for example, that the discovery of the act of bravery convinced Marius of the goodness of this man whom he had rejected as an exconvict. But compare this with the bishop, who needed no signs of virtue. To him Jean Valjean was a brother, and he welcomed him out of the caverns of darkness.

All for a loaf of bread, and to feed young and hungry mouths. That is the message to be remembered. That, and the relentless pursuit by one's past, the haunting memory of the secret life, from which there is so little hope of escape so long as men live in darkness and in ignorance. And they do, and they will.

NOTES

1. There is not a vast literature on the falsely accused. However, it is a theme worth studying as it has been adumbrated in the novel. A few pieces of fiction do come to mind: Tolstoi's *Resurrection* (discussed later in this essay) and several of Faulkner's novels, including *Intruder in the Dust, Light in August,* and—as pointed out in the essay on Temple Drake in this book—*Sanctuary.*

2. Lytton Strachey, *Landmarks in French Literature* (New York: Oxford University Press, 1969), p. 115. (First published in 1912.)

3. The entire scheme of charging that one man is someone else may be difficult for a modern reader to fathom. However, before identification by fingerprints, photography, and other means, it was a common event in Europe for a criminal to change his identity and, if rearrested, deny any criminal history or record.

4. André Maurois, Introduction to the Heritage Press edition, pp. xiv–xv.

5. Ibid., p. xv. The phrase quoted by Maurois is from Spinoza.

6. The concealed and the unconcealed (and often unconcealable) stigmas are discussed by Erving Goffman, in *Stigma: Notes on the Management of Spoiled Identity* (Englewood Cliffs, N.J.: Prentice-Hall, 1963). Goffman uses the terms "discredited" and "discreditable" to distinguish those whose stigma is known from those where it is still unknown. These are not exactly the same as the distinction made here between concealable and unconcealable, because sometimes a stigma can be hidden but is nevertheless made public.

7. There is a rich literature on escapes in coffins. Ethel Vance, in an anti-Nazi adventure novel, *Escape,* has her central character slip from the clutches of pursuing Fascists by leaving the country in a coffin. In *The Room in the Dragon Volant,* by Joseph Sheridan Le Fanu, a young man is drugged and placed in a coffin by a gang of thieves. In one of Arthur Schnitzler's short novels, *The Prophecy,* the central incident revolves around a living person in a coffin (it is a play that is being presented, not an escape). A variation on this occurs in Michael Crichton's fictionalized version of the sensational London robbery of gold in 1855, *The Great Train Robbery:* here one of the accomplices to the crime is smuggled on to the train in a coffin, pretending to be dead.

8. Arthur Waldhorn, "The Novel: 19th Century Continental," in J. Sherwood Weber, *Good Reading* (New York: Bowker, 1960), p. 91.

9. David Evans, *Social Romanticism in France, 1830–1848* (Oxford: At the Clarendon Press, 1951), p. 35.

10. Paul Berret, *Victor Hugo* (Paris: Garnier, 1927), p. 423, cited by Evans, ibid., p. 35.

11. David Evans, ibid., p. 36.

12. Leo Tolstoi, *Resurrection,* trans. Vera Traill (New York: New American Library, 1961), pp. 427–428.

13. Ibid., p. 428.

14. Ibid.

15. Doing the right act for the wrong reason is an interesting theme on which modern existentialists have focused their attention. See particularly a play by Jean-Paul Sartre, *Les Mains Sales (Dirty Hands).*

5

LORD JIM
In Endless Search
of Redemption

Of all the tormented figures in literature, from Oedipus the King through Hamlet and down to the tortured replications and reflections of self created by Eugene O'Neill, few are more tragic than the sailor depicted by Joseph Conrad, the chief mate known only as Jim, who is elevated to a lord by the natives who adopted him and with whom he finds, for a time, refuge and peace. A flaw with which all persons can identify is present in Lord Jim. He errs not merely in judgment and calculation, but in making a moral decision. In the most significant test he is ever to encounter, he finds himself on—one hesitates to say that he chooses—the path of cowardice rather than courage, expedience rather than principle, self-preservation rather than selflessness, treason rather than duty: in short, the immoral and not the moral in which he had ostensibly been reared by his parents in a country parsonage.

Jim's is a major error for which he cannot find excuse in youth or mitigation in inexperience, for it is committed in the mature years of his early manhood. The punishment, the official decree, meted out to him hardly seems to reflect—not only from the viewpoint of contemporary standards, but even those of retrospective years—the enormity with which his crime is regarded, both by himself and by other seamen. His certificate of seamanship is revoked. Thereupon, he inflicts on himself a

---

All quotations without notes are from Joseph Conrad, *Lord Jim* (New York: Doubleday, 1920).

far greater punishment, the self-torture of a man haunted by a past in which he has perpetrated an unforgivable deed. He spends the ensuing years in a dual pursuit. First, he seeks to escape from the memory of his deed, to wipe it out so to speak, and to live as if it had never occurred— an impossible task, and only made the more unbearable whenever he finds himself in the presence of someone who shares his secret (save for those who become father figures and befriend him). Then, further, he must prove his own worth to himself, to gain redemption, to convince himself of his own courage, to expiate his sin. There is, then, an ambiguity running through his life after the turning point in his career: he yearns both to escape and to believe in himself. Whether he succeeds in the struggle for redemption is problematic; it depends largely on the interpretation that the reader gives to the final episodes and the final passages of the book.

That Joseph Conrad intended *Lord Jim* to be an affirmation of his faith in man, that mankind can be redeemed, seems evident from his autobiography, a preface he wrote for the book, and other clues. Yet not all readers will find the reassurance in the book that its creator apparently wished to offer. For those who do, *Lord Jim,* more than anything written some decades later by William Faulkner (who in so many respects resembled Conrad), seems to express substantiation for the words of the Nobel Laureate when he said, in the face of a lifetime of writing to the contrary, that he had faith that mankind would endure and prevail.

All that is important in Jim's life is narrated by Marlow, through whom Conrad so intimately expressed his concerns for the fate of both Jim and humanity. With studied and deliberate repetition, Marlow assures us that Jim is hardly an ordinary person. He is made of better stuff than the rest of us, Marlow reiterates, with an affectionate and paternal love and with infinite compassion for one in his suffering; it is as if Marlow is urging the reader to believe it (or the listener, the audience to whom the story is told) in the face of so much evidence to the contrary. Jim is better, not worse, and it is this, the finer metal from which he is molded, that gives both torture and meaning to his life. There would have been no story, no suffering, no escape from the ineffable past and no endless search for the ever-eluctable hope for a second opportunity in which he would be redeemed, had Jim decided, as did at least one of the others in the lifeboat with him, to shrug the entire incident off, to throw it out of his mind, and to go off somewhere and start anew. To go off, yes; to start again, this he could and would have to do, but not without the burden of the past hanging over him, and the hope that some day he would be given an opportunity to prove himself a man of courage, not cowardice.

Yet, Marlow's protestations notwithstanding, Jim has many ordinary traits, although some extraordinary ones as well. If he were not an ordinary mortal whose crime could have been perpetrated by any of us, then the almost universal ability to identify with him in the suffering that followed would be absent. He does not have heroic proportions as much as he has heroic aspirations for himself and seeks to have heroic self-images. The latter do not derive from pathological disturbances and ensuing needs for reassurance; rather, they are aspirations that originate in the inner demand for expiation. It is in his dogged unwillingness and his unbending inability to live with the memory and the reminders of an act of weakness and cowardice, unless he first proves his self-worth through complete redemption, that he assumes extraordinary dimensions.

He is very human, in the sense in which that word is so often used to describe the frailties of humanity. In the great crisis in which he makes the fateful error that is to leave the mark of Cain upon him, he not only commits the cowardly act, as many would do, but goes to tortuous lengths to avoid responsibility for it. In fact, he did not do it, as Marlow relates the story and as Jim sees it; rather, it is something that happened to him.

The crucial event in Jim's life occurs when he is chief mate of the *Patna*. Jim and the other living officers—all white—abandon their ship with its human cargo, eight hundred sleeping natives, leaving them to their fate, a seemingly inevitable death soon to engulf them. Ostensibly, as the officers watch from the lifeboat, the lights on board the ship disappear, and then, so far as they can see in the darkness of night, the large vessel itself plunges into the sea, and all that the men now have to do is to concoct a story to explain their own escape. Jim sits among them in the lifeboat, the uninvited outsider, not wanted by the others, and Jim is already uncertain as to how much of their story he will be willing to corroborate. "Like the surviving officers of the *Patna*," writes J. I. Stewart, evoking the symbolism which appears to pervade Conrad, "we are all in the same boat."[1] But in what sense—of having fallen from grace, and of thus effacing the distinctions that separate us from others whose similar actions have not brought deep wounds of their conscience?

The scene in which Jim abandons the ship, unveiled by Marlow with suspense, structured circumlocution, and highly designed procrastination, capturing the hesitation, trepidation, doubts, second thoughts, and regrets of Jim himself, reveals both the strengths and weaknesses of the man, but the latter more than the former. He is not particularly liked by the other white officers, and one gets the impression that it is not any moral or intellectual superiority in Jim that separates him from

the others, but rather their moral inferiority. But is it not so that to say
one is to say the other? Not quite, for these are standards that the
reader judges against himself and his vision of humanity, and not
merely of Jim against his three reluctant companions. In the disaster
that the *Patna* meets at sea, with virtual certainty that the ship will not
survive, that it will be sinking within a few moments, the officers decide
that there is not time to wake the passengers, man the lifeboats, and
attempt to save those who can be rescued. Three officers lower a lifeboat and safely enter the water, and they call to a fourth to jump.
"George," they shout, they entreat, repeating his name, repeating the
word: Jump. But George is dead, apparently of a heart attack suffered
as the ship swayed and the debris flew and hit people and objects, and
as people were felled and fell. Jim is standing next to the dead seaman,
he thinks that he would like to go up and down the deck to ready the
lifeboats and awaken the sleeping cargo, but he is aware of the pressure
of time, the ship is about to be torn asunder and take its final plunge, he
hears the men below calling, calling to George, it is true, but calling
nonetheless, entreating him, or someone, to jump. George is dead. In
the darkness, and enveloped by the impending doom, he, Jim, loses his
own bearings, and he finds himself in the lifeboat.

He finds himself in the lifeboat. No, he does not jump, at least as
he tells the story and as Marlow repeats it, nor does he ever quite see it
that way himself. In the ultimate search for an escape from responsibility, in the inability to accept as a fact that he did what he did and not
that it was done to him, there is no act of jumping, but only the crisis
on board, the cries from below, and, as if by magic or miracle, the
intervening time is effaced and with it the onus of having made a
decision and deliberately taken a step. He is in the lifeboat; the others
are the ones who man a boat and put it into the sea, who call out to
someone on deck to jump, but Jim is the passive actor. Despised by
those who discover that it is not George but Jim who is now sharing
their fate in the lifeboat, Jim is hesitant about his own willingness to
become part of the conspiracy to conceal the crime, and he is already
morally distinguishing himself from his companions and from the act
that they had all committed, a distinction that he can make all the more
readily because, in his mind, he has not jumped into the boat, but finds
himself there.

Of the jump itself, David Daiches notes, "Jim will never admit that
it was a decision; it was something that happened to him." When he
does reluctantly admit culpability for the act, he does it with words and
in a way "that make the reader share Jim's sense of disbelief in his own
guilt," Daiches adds. "Yet the reader is aware at the same time that he
ought not to share this disbelief."[2] But perhaps, from the viewpoint of

criminal responsibility, a more relevant approach is an existential one, as stated succinctly by Edwin Moseley: "Whether he jumps compulsively or deliberately is beside the point. The fact remains that, like the amoral ones who have chosen to desert, Jim is guilty of jumping."[3]

Conrad's Jim has human weakness, as recapitulated in the moment of crisis: his incapacity to act decisively, his surrender to the coward within, the priority given to self-preservation rather than moral responsibility in the face of impending destruction. It does not end there, however, for his weakness is highlighted, not reduced, by his willingness to rearrange, blot out, and in other ways handle the past so that guilt is in some way mitigated, even if slightly.

The question is never raised by Conrad, but one can speculate whether Jim would have been equally haunted by the memory of abandonment, and whether he would in his own mind have defined his own act as cowardice, had the *Patna* not survived the squalls and storms that racked the sea. What if the plunge and descent so clearly seen in the night had been reality and not illusion of desperate men? Had the *Patna* taken to the ocean floor the secret of his treachery and that of the others, would the memory of that night and of the men, women, and children on that ship have followed him? It is doubtful, there is no evidence of it, or of Conrad's belief in it. In the end, is it not the discovery, the public humiliation, rather than the act itself, that hounds him through life? Without that the event might have been reduced to an incident, to be tucked away and seldom taken out, certainly not something that cannot ever leave him. In that sense, then, Jim is of ordinary and very human proportions: first, in the choice that he makes (for many would have made it, and readers can identify with it), then, in the machinations of his mind to avoid seeing it as choice, and finally in the nature of the guilt, with which he could survive if not for the reminder of it because it is known about by others. Without all of these elements, Conrad would be giving us a godlike rather than a manlike hero; these are foibles that plague all people, signs of the imperfections in humanity.

There is considerable ambiguity in Jim's character, and if it is a weakness of Jim's, it is a strength of Conrad's that one can find an arsenal of argument for a contrary view. One can point to a confrontation between Marlow and Jim in which the former shouts, "It is not I or the world who remembers," and continues, "It is you—you who remember" (p. 236). But just what is it that Jim remembers, the act of cowardice or the public ignominy? It appears to be a wavering, first one and then the other, but even more an interweaving. What I am suggesting here is that there is no evidence offered by Conrad that Jim would have been haunted by his own evil and driven to death in search of redemption had the knowledge of his failure remained buried only within him, or even shared by a few culprits. In that sense, then, he is as weak as humanity itself, and is never the heroic figure who has on a lone occasion faltered. This dilemma in the portrait of Jim is left to the reader to unravel and interpret; it is the reader's ultimate task, in the words of the critic Albert J. Guerard, "to locate this vulnerable idealist and conscientious failure on a moral spectrum. He [the reader] must decide whether Jim's is a drama of bruised vanity or a tragedy of conscience."4

Marlow first meets Jim at the hearings, the inquiry into the *Patna* affair which, in the age of Britain's hegemony over the seas and her paternalistic protective covering for native peoples which concealed imperialist oppression, cast a blight over British honor. Jim is attending the hearings, the only lifeboat survivor present, as David Daiches notes. The others have run away. "But is his remaining to face the inquiry," asks Daiches, "a sign of grace or a sign of false romanticism? Is he as different from the other two guilty men as he imagines? Is he really running away when he thinks he is facing it out?"5

These are probably not questions going through the mind of Marlow, as he sits, taken by the younger man, touched by his despondency, by his desperate effort to cling to some shred of belief in his own honor and pride, and not to think of himself as the man who was a coward in the *Patna* affair. The escape from responsibility is a part of this, but it is not enough; now he must escape from a world that points the finger of scorn at him. With Marlow's aid, at first arrogantly repulsed and later accepted, he is found a post, a place where no one will suspect the blight upon his record. There he works well, with a certain insouciance, an ability to lose himself in the daily tasks which he performs with superb dedication. If he is not redeemed, he is at least able to forget.

It is one of many jobs in different places that Jim takes, running from one port to another, a fugitive from his own biography. Marlow tells how three of these episodes come to their end.

In one instance, a man who is working at the local factory turns out to be one of his companions in the ill-fated journey in the lifeboat. He cannot look at this factory hand, and worse, Jim's erstwhile comrade says that he knows why Jim is there. So, with neither warning nor notice, and to the dismay of an employer who has developed a fondness for and dependency on him, Jim gets up and leaves, on to another spot. There were no spoons missing, the host tells Marlow.

The incident is part of a pattern. On another occasion, Jim is well entrenched in a new position, under a new identity. One day, again without notice, he announces that he is resigning and will be on his way. Was anything said about the *Patna*, Marlow asks the employer, and indeed, come to think of it, something was. Jim was having a sandwich in a room in which a large group of men of the sea were standing around a telescope watching a steamer come in; their talk turned to the *Patna* and someone said that what had happened there was "a disgrace to human natur'" and that the men who had abandoned the ship were skunks. Upon which one of the men remarked, "It stinks here now." That day Jim left his job.

Marlow owes the employer an explanation, and he gives it, in the simplest words, stating no more than that Jim was one of the men who had abandoned the *Patna*. The other is surprised, even shocked, but immediately recovers to ask: But what difference would that have made?

In a third episode which Marlow describes, and the three are meant to summarize an almost endless series of incidents, many people appear to know about Jim, but there is a conspiracy of silence. Perhaps he suspects that his history is known, but he is protected by the delicacy of others and the illusions that a human being can conjure to protect himself. Jim is in a billiards game and an argument breaks out; his adversary says something—one can only guess that it had to do with his special area of sensitivity—and Jim breaks a cue and bodily lifts the other man and throws him from a veranda into the river below. Hardly the act of an English gentleman, and again Jim is on his way.

The three incidents have elements of similarity and difference. In the first, Jim has to face an accomplice in cowardice who does not condemn but conspires to condone. The secret would have remained, the exposure that he dreaded need not have happened, but he could not face the reminder, particularly in the form of someone who symbolized for him what was most despicable about himself. In the second, an officer thunders his contempt, but no one knows that it is against Jim, and even after Jim has departed, no rumors to that effect have reached those he left behind. In the third, he is surrounded by a world that knows but protects him from knowledge of that knowledge, a protection disrupted in a moment of what might have been a trivial dispute, had it not aroused in him an explosion of anger.

In these and other incidents, Jim is displaying an inability to be in the presence of anyone who knows: an indifferent bystander, a corrupt accomplice, a vengeful judge, a forgiving and accepting employer. The key to Jim's long odyssey, which is going to take him through to the last days of his life, is not redemption, or even self-image: it is mirror-image. What is unbearable is not so much the memory of what he has done, but the reminder of it—without the reminder, he might almost forget. At times, and haltingly, he appears to be able to live with himself, without erasing the *Patna* from the consciousness of his life history, but he cannot live in the presence of others who know, no matter who they are and what attitudes they take (even Marlow and later Stein are not exceptions). The unresolved issue of self-reflection in Jim's life is that he cannot decide whether he is fleeing from the act and the awareness of his own cowardice, or from those who know about it, or finally from a conscience that tells him that he has done wrong.

In Conrad's vision, it is how a man sees himself that will determine his ability to cope with the travails of life. In Jim's view of the world, it is how he is seen by others that will determine his fate. In the world of social psychology, the two are synthesized: it is not so much how Jim sees himself that is crucial (although there is a good deal of this) nor how he is seen by others, but how Jim sees others seeing him. A person cannot have a secret from himself, but he cannot allow himself to know that the concealed and discredited parts of his being are known to another, or to the world out there.

All of which leads us to Patusan. Marlow has to find a place for Jim, as he has sought to do on so many occasions in the past. He approaches Stein, a connoisseur who collects beetles and butterflies, does commerce with the natives, and has established trading posts in spots inaccessible, never visited (or seldom, at least) by white men. Such a place is Patusan. There, with all of the difficulties and dangers, the native rivalries in which one can easily get caught, there is little chance that an unassuming young Englishman will ever come to the attention of curious eyes that will penetrate into his most private past.

One is not quite sure of the location of Patusan. It is somewhere in Southeast Asia, the name of Haiphong is mentioned, and there are Malayans, but it is its almost complete inaccessibility, not its geography, that is of significance. Jim accepts the assignment. There are many problems that he will enounter: rival factions among the natives in Patusan, and another employee, one Cornelius, who will be discharged from his post and will surely line up as an enemy of Jim. The very first day, Jim is caught up in the native rivalry, comes close to being held prisoner and possibly killed, but escapes and reaches his destination. After presenting himself to the native ruler, Doramin, an incredibly obese man who has literally to be carried in a chair because he is unable to move about by himself, Jim meets Dain Waris, who never emerges as a character in his own right but only as the son of Doramin and friend of Jim (it is one of the few instances in the book where the role relationships are developed at the expense of the credibility of the person). It is in Patusan that Jim's leadership of the community brings forth such reverence that he becomes known as Tuan Jim, the name given to him by the natives and from which the title of the book is taken. The faith in his integrity and in his judgment is unequalled and unchallenged. He can never waver. But he is chasing a dream, like Stein running after a rare specimen of a butterfly, the romantic notion that another occasion as demanding as the *Patna* will present itself, and that he will be able to prove to himself that he is courageous and not cowardly. Without this new opportunity, Jim is unfulfilled. The void in his life is not going to disappear, although he now has a love in Patusan, a girl whom he calls Jewel (giving rise to rumors of a large and priceless emerald that the white man has found). She is the daughter of a native woman who died soon after her white lover abandoned her, and her stepfather is Cornelius, a man filled with greed, hatred, jealousy, and resentment.

Tuan Jim discovers the last outpost on earth, and in it he comes as close to finding inner peace as is within his capacities and his history. That he can never forget why he has come to Patusan is indisputable, but the good life he is living and the positive benefits he is bringing to the natives (a sort of secular missionary, with no venal or otherworldly motives or imperialist connections) give him some element of redeeming worth. Above all, no one knows or can know, nor can one suspect, why he is among them. When Jewel, so fearful that one day he will leave the way her father had left her mother, and as white men eventually do, is reassured that Jim will never depart (the reassurance is given her by Marlow on one of his periodic visits), she demands to know why. Marlow says it is because Jim is not good enough, and Jewel hurls back a few words that reveal her adoration and admiration, as well as the searing insecurity of the relationship: that this is a lie. However, she expresses her bewilderment when she discloses that it is the same lie that Jim has told her.

Jewel asks Marlow never to return, she wants no more association between Jim and the outside world lest he be tempted to leave, and Marlow does bid farewell, both to Jewel and to Jim. In what will be their last meeting and their last parting, Jim starts to give Marlow a message, to tell them, out there . . . and then he stops. The message is undisclosed, and the reader is left to conjecture even as Marlow does. Yet it appears that the answer lies in Jim's hesitation and then cessation—Jim still does not know what the message of his life has been. He is still searching, building castles in the air, waiting for a new opportunity, and uncertain as to his own feelings about the man who abandoned the *Patna*. For the moment, it is the end of Marlow's narration.

Jim might have lived out the rest of his natural life in Patusan, perhaps another thirty or forty years or so, all with Jewel and possibly a family as well, in the place where he need not fear the arrival of someone who would recognize him and where he might find the peaceful existence of a new life. He does want another chance, a new opportunity, a second crisis in which he can prove to himself that he is a man of valor, but lacking this he will compromise by settling for a world in which he is held in the highest esteem by people whose faith in that courage is undoubting and whose knowledge of his past is nil. It is almost as if this past does not exist; almost, yet not quite, for without the past, Jim would not have been inextricably bound to Patusan or to Jewel. One might dispute that he remains because he is not good enough, but the statement can hardly be denied when it is placed in subjective terms: he remains because he envisages himself as not being good enough. If he is not quite satisfied with what Patusan has to offer, it is only because the opportunity for self-validation, complete expiation, and redemption has not presented itself.

In many ways, Patusan is too idyllic to be a place of suffering or even exile for the grave sin that Jim has committed. One can envy everything about Jim's last years except the torture within. The world which he inhabits has since vanished and perhaps it never was, for when the white men came to the native places (as Joseph Conrad so well knew and so explicitly stated), it was not with benevolent Jims, but with exploiters, false gods, slave runners, whiskey, new diseases, bullets, and the other amenities of civilization. The natives were lucky with Jim, but not so lucky as he with them, among whom he found a happiness that is hardly the just deserts of the sinner.

Thus Jim approaches the brink of an inner peace in a life among people who believe in him, and if there is no absolution for the sin of his youth, there is concealment so effective that he need no longer face each day the fear that he will look up to see, in the stare of another, the suspicion if not the outright contempt of those who know about him. Patusan is the last place to go. It is literally and symbolically the most inaccessible territory, from which there can be no further escape. Temple Drake's son, in *Requiem for a Nun,* will ask her where they are going to run after the execution, and she knows that there is no further bus stop or airport. For Jim, it is the same: after another disclosure, or another failure, there can be no further boatstops. He has run and run and has come to the point where, like a trapped animal, there will be no other place to which to retreat. Yet not quite like a trapped animal, for he has a degree of contentment here; he has come as close to serenity as the burden of his memory will permit.

Romantic that he is, as Marlow so frequently informs his audience, Jim still dreams of another opportunity to disprove to himself what both he and Marlow have said to Jewel, that he is not good enough. In short, he seeks redemption. Yet it must have pleased the romantic within him to see himself as Tuan Jim, to be addressed with love and reverence, and to know that he neither patronized nor exploited the people of Patusan.[6] In the inner self, the struggle to attain expiation, atonement, and repurification must have an ending, in success or failure; without it Jim leads only a life that many in the world out there would exchange for their own. In this sense, then, he does not suffer in Patusan; using the word in other than its economic meaning, he comes near to prospering.

That is where Marlow leaves the story, with Jim's secret unknown, closely guarded even from the woman he loves and from his friend Dain Waris. Marlow has broken all association with the young man he had first met at the inquiry into the desertion of the *Patna*. He has made a commitment to Jewel never to return, and he too might have ended his years without ever hearing again of the man who found some hope of resurrection in a self-imposed exile. But although Marlow does not return, details of the final episode in the life of Jim do reach him.

Word of Patusan, isolated and almost inaccessible retreat, has spread; the land is known to traders who would exploit it, perhaps to adventurers and explorers who might be curious about it, to outlaws who would use it as a sanctuary. Among the latter is a miserable band of pirate seamen led by the fugitive Gentleman Brown (one has only to recall the special meaning given by the English, especially at the turn of the century, to the word *gentleman* to appreciate the irony). Brown is wanted by the authorities on many charges. Desperate for food and booty, he and his men navigate their way to within a short distance of Jim's village, ready to plunder the whole area, undeterred by any reluctance to kill the natives. But they meet unexpected resistance.

Jim is away, off somewhere in the forests, and not expected to return for about seven days; natives are sent in many directions in search of him, for his counsel, his leadership, and his wisdom in the struggle to defend the village against the white intruders. Meanwhile, Dain Waris and a group of his men are sent to a strategic position where they will be able to attack Brown's miniature navy should this be necessary for defense of their people. Cornelius, Jewel's one-time foster father, the man whom Jim displaced in Stein's trading post and who, in his greed, vainly tried to exact a bride-price for the girl, only to be rebuffed, now makes contact with Brown. Cornelius in effect joins the enemy, giving counsel and advice to the intruders on how they can attack, plunder, and escape.

When Brown sees that he is unable to storm the village, he decides that the only alternative is to make a retreat, and his main problem is how to effect this without being slaughtered. It is at this point that Jim returns, and in a dramatic meeting with Brown, the white lord of Patusan asks the invaders to disarm and to leave the area, promising them safe passage. Brown is puzzled by Jim, does not pretend to understand him, and in the bargaining says that a life is a life, and that he will fight for his:

When he asked Jim, with a sort of brusque despairing frankness, whether he himself—straight now—didn't understand that when "it came to saving one's life in the dark, one didn't care who else went—three, thirty, three hundred people"—it was as if a demon had been whispering advice in his ear. "I made him wince," boasted Brown to me. [The letter is from Stein to Marlow.] (Pp. 386–387)

The reference to saving one's life in the dark is reminiscent of an earlier passage, when an employer, trying to convince Jim not to leave, says of their business that their ship is not going to sink. It illustrates the precarious existence of all those living with a tightly held secret, the startling reaction evoked when the most innocent word or phrase is given a meaning other than that intended, touching the most sensitive nervesystem, eliciting fear, suspicion, belief that the edifice so carefully structured is about to tumble.[7]

Brown has evidently found the weakness in Jim, and is pursuing it; in his desperation, he is going to exploit it to the utmost:

He asked Jim whether he had nothing fishy in his life to remember that he was so damnedly hard upon a man trying to get out of a deadly hole by the first means that came to hand—and so on, and so on. And there ran through the rough talk a vein of subtle reference to their common blood, an assumption of common experience; a sickening suggestion of common guilt, of secret knowledge that was like a bond of their minds and of their hearts. (P. 387)

Jim relents, he will return to the people of Patusan and urge that the invaders be permitted free passage without being disarmed. He goes back to Doramin, has a council meeting, pleads for acceptance of the position he has taken, and obtains compliance. Word is sent to Dain Waris by messenger not to fire upon the ship that is retreating.

Through the combined efforts of Cornelius and Brown, the agreement is betrayed. Unprepared for an attack, Dain Waris's position is fired upon by the retreating ship, and Brown escapes, leaving behind the dead body of Dain Waris, friend of Jim and son of Doramin. The body of the slain friend is brought to the grieving parents while a messenger brings the news to Jim, alone in his house with Jewel and his manservant, Tamb' Itam. Jewel desperately begs Jim not to leave the house, not to go to the body, to run away with her, to run anywhere, just to make an escape. She does not know that that is what Jim has been doing all of his adult life, endlessly running, searching for new avenues of escape, and that now there is no place left to which he can go. There will not be another Patusan. There is an even more important reason that Jim cannot leave: this is the *Patna* again, and he will not show his cowardice by slinking away in the face of danger.

To the natives, and no doubt to himself as well, he has made a grave miscalculation. In their minds it may be nothing short of betrayal, but whether it is treachery that their lord has committed or merely an error, it has the same effect, needless deaths which could have been averted had Brown's trapped boat been disarmed and not given free and safe passage. For Jim it is the end of the road, not merely because there is no further place to which he can escape, something he must know all too well, but also because this is his second failure. He was given another chance, and he showed judgment as bad in this instance as in the first. Only it is now different. Nobody told him to make the error (as in the *Patna* episode); he cannot describe it in terms analogous to finding himself in the boat. He made the decision, with premeditation and calculation, and it fell entirely on his shoulders; more than that, it was he, Jim, who convinced Doramin and the council to go along with the fateful error. He will leave the house not through a back door but standing upright and with courage, to face Doramin. All of Jewel's entreaties are without avail.

Surely he must have known that he was going to his death, but how it must have appealed to the romantic within him that he had found an opportunity to redeem himself, accept responsibility, recapture faith in his own courage and heroism, by walking fearlessly toward the ultimate in self-sacrifice. His was a knowledge that he had acted righteously and in good faith, that he had betrayed no one, and even if that knowledge was no longer shared by his immediate world, the belief in self was firm.

What thoughts passed through his head—what memories? Who can tell? Everything was gone, and he who had been once unfaithful to his trust had lost again all men's confidence. It was then, I believe, he tried to write—to somebody—and gave it up. Loneliness was closing on him. People had trusted him with their lives—only for that; and yet they could never, as he had said, never be made to understand him. Those without did not hear him make a sound. Later, towards the evening, he came to the door and called for Tamb' Itam. "Well?" he asked. "There is much weeping. Much anger, too," said Tamb' Itam. Jim looked up at him. "You know," he murmured. "Yes, Tuan," said Tamb' Itam. "Thy servant does know, and the gates are closed. We shall have to fight." "Fight! What for?" he asked. "For our lives." "I have no life," he said. Tamb' Itam heard a cry from the girl at the door. "Who knows?" said Tamb' Itam. "By audacity and cunning we may even escape. There is much fear in men's hearts, too." He went out, thinking vaguely of boats and of open sea, leaving Jim and the girl together. (P. 409)

There is no open sea, there is no escape, there is no life. It is not something that Tamb' Itam or Jewel could have known, for he had been unable through their years together to make himself reveal this to either of them, nor to his friend who is now dead. Who could know that once he had been unfaithful in the call of duty, and who but himself could know that this time he has not been unfaithful, although the belief in his treachery is pervasive? If on the night of the *Patna* he had betrayed the confidence that mankind had placed in him and had compromised his own moral commitments, albeit in a manner that sought to shift much of the blame elsewhere, this time he can hold himself high in self-esteem. He has been victimized by the faith that he had in another man, and betrayed by that misplaced trust; trapped in part by the man's probing into something mysterious in Jim's past, he made a wrong decision, resulting in a fatality all the more terrible because he who was killed was one with whom he had, in Marlow's words, a "strange, profound, rare friendship." That he has again lost all men's confidence no one can gainsay, and nothing is so dear to him as to feel that there is deserved trust in him among his fellowmen. He has spent years building, nurturing, cherishing it, and in one stroke of a bullet, it is gone. There are no more men to run to in order to build a community of people with confidence in him; instead, there are now two terrible memories of failure, not one, from which to flee.

Jewel asks him to fight, but he says there is nothing to fight for; she asks him to flee, and he says there is no escape. She reminds him that he had promised that he would never leave, that he had promised unasked, does he not remember, to which he replies: "I should not be worth having." He leaves and goes to Doramin and the mourning party:

> "He came! He came!" was running from lip to lip, making a murmur to which he moved. "He hath taken it upon his own head," a· voice said aloud. He heard this and turned to the crowd. "Yes. Upon my head." A few people recoiled. Jim waited awhile before Doramin, and then said gently, "I am come in sorrow." He waited again. "I am come ready and unarmed," he repeated. (P. 415)

Doramin raises his hand and shoots. In what may be the most important key to an understanding of Jim and of Conrad, the death is described in a few simple words: "They say that the white man sent right and left at all those faces a proud and unflinching glance. Then with his hand over his lips he fell forward, dead" (p. 416).

Of what was he proud and what was demonstrated by his unflinching glance? For the last time Marlow, the voice of Conrad, speaks to the reader:

And that's the end. He passes away under a cloud, inscrutable at heart, forgotten, unforgiven, and excessively romantic. Not in the wildest days of his boyish visions could he have seen the alluring shape of such an extraordinary success! For it may very well be that in the short moment of his last proud and unflinching glance, he had beheld the face of that opportunity which, like an Eastern bride, had come veiled to his side. (P. 416)

That he died knowing that he was a man of courage cannot be denied. In Conrad's words about the character he created, Jim was a man in search of lost honor, and if his lifelong struggle is to be seen in these terms, he regained it, because in the end the honor that counts—as Jim could never accept until the last day of his life—is the way a human being views himself. All of his life he had been concerned because, the efforts to escape responsibility notwithstanding, he knew within that his had been an act of cowardice, that there was no defense for it. The excuses that he was able to construct for the *Patna* episode were insufficient, and his fugitive life, hiding not from law but from humanity, from the knowing eyes of those to whom his secret, and with it his innermost being, had been revealed, was a façade. Even in Patusan, surrounded by those who gave him love and trust, he could not escape from the haunting past, harboring the ever-present suspicion that the trust of those who called him Tuan Jim was founded in their ignorance of his buried life. I am not good enough, he tells Jewel, and to others he tells nothing at all.

Redemption for Jim is an inner struggle. No one's innards can be revealed, everyone has dark secrets that cannot be bared even to one's intimates. They are seldom secrets, however, that the bearer is aware of, recognizes, and carries around in his consciousness; they do not pound upon him daily, urging him to flee to people and to places where the secrets are unshared.

Albert Guerard maintains that it is not Jim's romantic search for lost honor, his inner struggle for redemption, that shapes the climax of the book (and of his life), but his indecision, his unconscious inability to function under stress:

For Jim is literally immobilized at the critical moments of his life. As a boy on the training-ship he cannot move and loses his chance to join the rescue. On board the *Patna* the conscious man stands still for twenty-seven minutes, till something less than consciousness makes him jump . . . into an immobilizing guilt, an everlasting black hole. Thereafter he is paralyzed by all chance reminders of the *Patna* incident. His inability to act—his immobilization by his "double" Gentleman Brown—brings on the catastrophe.[8]

This is hardly the description of a man whose author describes his life as one in search of lost honor. The failure to act for twenty-seven minutes on the *Patna* is the indecision of one who is searching to make a moral decision, and who then allows it to be made for him. He is never immobilized when the *Patna* is mentioned: he picks himself up and goes elsewhere, no more immobile than an army in retreat, or an escaped convict dashing from one hideout to another. He is not immobilized by Brown: on the contrary, he takes action, but it is the wrong action, and his suicidal walk into the gunrange of Doramin at the end is an expression that this is not the *Patna* again; it is its very reverse, the certainty in his own mind that he has taken the moral, honorable, and courageous path, and that he can die having been made whole by this knowledge.

Guerard's contention that Brown is Jim's double focuses on a key relationship. The theme of the double held a fascination for Conrad, as it did for Dostoevsky (it is particularly striking in Conrad's *The Secret Sharer* and in Dostoevsky's story "The Double") and one might speculate that Jim sees in Brown the mirror of all that he perceives and hates in himself. However, Conrad's characterization of Jim as a man in search of his lost honor, ready to die (and in fact dying) to retrieve it, is in contrast to his depiction of Brown as a man of dishonor. To believe that Jim sees himself in Brown is possible only if one accepts the depths of self-abnegation and self-flagellation of the mate of the *Patna,* but even this distinguishes the two men, for the sufferings of guilt require the recognition of wrong and the aspirations to become a person of probity and integrity that were beyond Brown but were a part of Jim's entire being.

David Daiches also sees the relationship between Lord Jim and Gentleman Brown as a pivotal, symbolic one. Lord Jim is destroyed because, "perpetually immature, he refuses to recognize the kinship claimed by Gentleman Brown, the kinship with evil; but the kinship, however superficially remote, is really there, and to fight it is to invite self-destruction." In another passage, Daiches contends that Jim, after unintentionally betraying his people "because he accepts the blackmail of identification between Brown and himself . . . makes amends to *himself* by going to his certain and useless death in a gesture of purely romantic histrionics. Is this his ultimate vindication or his ultimate failure?"[9] (Emphasis in original)

It is a certain death, true, but whether it is useless might be argued. Jim is proud in his moment of death. He faces death with pride not only because he has not fled, rejecting the route that he had chosen before, but because by going to his death he has found redemption. In death is expiation; to pay for one's transgressions is to be made whole again. He alone knows that the trust placed in him was not misdirected, that it was not given to a man without honor who misused and abused it; and that knowledge, which he had sought to attain about himself all of his life, is sufficient to infuse the suicidal act with pride. Suddenly, in his most genuine moment of sorrow, standing by the side of bereaved parents and himself grieving for a friend who has died by his error and none other, he retrieves his faith in self and he can die knowing that he has not sought redemption in vain. That he is unflinching is not only a matter of determination, a symbolic statement that no other path can be considered, but an affirmation that he goes to death convinced that he possesses the courage that he has so long sought to find within himself, and whose existence he has for long years doubted.[10]

C. B. Cox writes that Jim's decision to die "results from a consciousness of his own unworthiness." If this is so, and if all humanity is represented by Jim, who—as we are constantly reminded—is one of us, then this raises further questions. Cox continues: "Is all human activity a sham, only acceptable to the deluded and the hypocritical? Is the man who commits suicide the man who sees most?" And finally: "*Lord Jim* dramatizes the claims both of a complete moral nihilism and a commitment to ideals of service to the community; the novel never rests finally in any decisive posture."[11]

How much Conrad saw that Jim, an anonymous person whose last name is never revealed, thus being at the same time a nobody and everybody, is all humanity, is indicated in the closing words of an Author's Note written for the novel in 1917, some seventeen years after publication of the book:

> One sunny morning in the commonplace surroundings of an Eastern road-stead, I saw his form pass by—appealing—significant—under a cloud—perfectly silent. Which is as it should be. It was for me, with all the sympathy of which I was capable, to seek fit words for his meaning. He was "one of us." (P. ix)

Jim takes the fall (a passive word, unlike jump), and it is a recapitulation of the fall that all humanity has taken, since the first transgression by Adam. It was of Adam that Søren Kierkegaard wrote: "For how could he have understood the difference between good and evil, seeing that this distinction was in fact consequent upon the enjoyment of the fruit?"[12] It is not within the province of Jim, and the millions of others who have come after Adam, to have such exculpatory apologetics, for they (read *we*) could have understood this difference, having learned by the errors of Adam. For Adam, evil was a fruit to be enjoyed, but only with banishment as the symbol of suffering for having tasted it. The analogy with Jim is apparent: the enjoyment was in saving his own life, the banishment is literal and self-imposed. Adam placed the blame upon the snake and upon Eve: there are always others, people or circumstances, for those who search.

Jim has made a lifelong effort to diminish guilt, by denying it to himself (the escape from responsibility) and by refusing to face all others who know of it (the escape from tormentors). But it is only through guilt that one can recognize that once he was innocent. Again, as Kierkegaard so profoundly puts it:

> As Adam lost innocence by guilt, so does every man lose it. If it was not by guilt he lost it, neither was it innocence he lost; and if he was not innocent before he became guilty, he never became guilty.[13]

Only in the final hours of his life does Jim accept responsibility for the action that has led to his friend's death, and in accepting it, he likewise affirms, if only by implication, that he was responsible for the decision to jump. He can face death unflinchingly because it is with courage reborn. It is courage that he has been seeking to discover in himself since the abandonment of the *Patna;* and he can go with pride to Doramin in what will be the last moment of his life because he has been redeemed in his own eyes, even if, with infinite irony, this takes place through the act of destroying the faith that others have had in him. Kierkegaard again offers an insight into the life and death of Lord Jim:

> But only by guilt is innocence lost; every man loses innocence in essentially the same way that Adam did, and it is not in the interest of ethics to represent all men as troubled and interested spectators of guilt, but not guilty, nor is it to the interest of dogmatics to represent all as interested and sympathetic spectators of redemption, but not redeemed.[14]

Lord Jim was no interested spectator on the very sidelines of guilt, any more than he was on the sidelines of life. He was guilty, he had lost his innocence, and indeed in death he was redeemed.

NOTES

1. J. I. M. Stewart, *Joseph Conrad* (New York: Dodd, Mead, 1968), p. 110.
2. David Daiches, *The Novel and the Modern World,* rev. ed. (Chicago: University of Chicago Press, 1960), p. 34.
3. Edwin Moseley, *Pseudonyms of Christ in the Modern Novel: Motifs and Methods* (Pittsburgh: University of Pittsburgh Press, 1962), p. 28.

4. See Albert J. Guerard's Introduction to *Nostromo* in The Laurel Conrad (New York: Dell, 1960), p. 15.

5. Daiches, *The Novel*, p. 32. Incidentally, Daiches errs when he refers to the "other two guilty men," for there were three others in the lifeboat with Jim.

6. Guerard is not as generous in his evaluation of Jim's devotion to the people of Patusan: "The Lord Jim of Patusan is thus intoxicated by his power to do good, and his protection of the community at last brings it ruin. The vain dreamer may be possessed at last by what he thought to possess. . . . " (Introduction to *Nostromo*, p. 15). It can be argued, however, that it is not the protection that Jim offers Patusan that brings tragedy, nor even the natives' misplaced faith in him, but his own faith in the word of one who is utterly untrustworthy. Thus, the *Patna* was for Jim an error of moral transgression; later, in the event that is going to result in his death, misplaced trust was an error of judgment. The distinction had to be significant for him, because without it his death has no meaning.

7. Dostoevsky, in *Crime and Punishment*, makes masterly use of the effect of ambiguous and innocently dropped words and phrases on the mind of a man frightened by a possible disclosure. Almost every conversation in which Raskolnikov finds himself, or even overhears, during the days following the murders contains an element of hidden meaning telling him that he is suspected and is about to be apprehended, although actually it is his own startled reactions and interpretations of these words that arouse suspicion and serve as self-disclosures. Raskolnikov is driven by a simultaneous need to be found out and to protect himself from such an eventuality, whereas Jim's transgression is a secret that he has no inner need to share with any around him. What links the two is the torture of a man requiring expiation.

8. Guerard, Introduction to *Nostromo*, p. 15 (ellipses in original).

9. Daiches, *The Novel*, pp. 30–31, 32.

10. There are some interesting analogies between *Lord Jim* and a proletarian novel written by Sherwood Anderson, *Beyond Desire*. In Anderson's book, the hero, Red, endures a self-imposed "exile," but not for an act of cowardice or any transgression; rather it is a voluntary renunciation of his middle-class values and a manner of expressing solidarity with textile strikers. In the camp of the strikers he fails (or believes that he has failed), and when the strikers go forth to meet the sheriffs and the employers' hired thugs, and then retreat before their armed might, he steps forward to stop the first bullet. Like Jim, Anderson's Red was a romantic in search of redemption.

11. C. B. Cox, *Joseph Conrad: The Modern Imagination* (Totowa, N.J.: Rowman & Littlefield, 1974), p. 18.

12. Søren Kierkegaard, *The Concept of Dread*, trans. with an introduction and notes by Walter Lowrie (Princeton: Princeton University Press, 1946), p. 40.

13. Ibid., p. 32.

14. Ibid.

6

ETHAN FROME
Atonement Endures Until Darkness Descends

Although Edith Wharton was herself a product of upper-class America, which she described, satirized, and criticized, she ventured outside it to depict people struggling for existence in their barren, impoverished, and essentially hopeless lives. In *Ethan Frome* her characters are not the idle rich but the toiling poor, people who struggle for every penny, ordinary folk condemned to drudgery.

Alfred Kazin describes Wharton as having written of the lower class: "Whenever she wrote of that world, darkness and revulsion entered her work mechanically. She thought of the poor not as a class but as a condition; the qualities she automatically ascribed to the poor—drabness, meanness, anguish—became another manifestation of the futility of human effort."[1] Drabness, meanness, anguish: it would be difficult to find a work in American literature in which they are more prominent than in *Ethan Frome*. And futility of human effort? For the characters in this work, living cannot be other than futile. It is a world bereft of hope.

Yet, for a moment at least, two of these lower-class persons almost escape. They dare to let light shine into the darkness of their lives, although their crime, if it can be called that, their infidelity in hope and

All quotations without notes are from Edith Wharton, *Ethan Frome*, Scribner's Library Books (New York: Scribner, n.d.). Wherever ellipses appear, they are in the original, including those at the end of a quotation.

wish and dream but not in expectations or fulfillment, leads them to their doom. Add to the irony of Wharton's story, bitter and acerbic, this message: Suffer, without repentance, without hope, just suffer.

Among the belles lettres of crime and punishment, with their insights into the human mind and the human condition, *Ethan Frome* is a powerful work, almost unique; for, to use one of the endless plays on the three-word title inspired by Dostoevsky, it is punishment without crime; even more, it is suffering without hope of alleviation, atonement in which those caught in the tragedy will never be "at one" and hence can never complete their atonement. There is no redemption, nor can the three persons who make up the novel even reach out to be redeemed; rather, they forcefully epitomize the cruel reality that human beings are condemned to live. And they are condemned. The endless morrows can bring to the man and two women bound together in one life pattern and in one small house only the eternal and continuing and monotonous reliving each day of what so burdensomely had been lived through the day before. Is this the plight of humanity?

The reader meets Ethan Frome the man and *Ethan Frome* the novel through a narrator, one who unobtrusively enters the story only to leave it, nameless and yet not entirely without purpose. The narrator does not glide upon the scene so haphazardly as Wharton's casual style might lead us to believe: he (or she, perhaps this is Wharton herself; we do not know and it matters little) comes to a town where he meets a new world of strangers, and he is attracted, puzzled, emotionally and cerebrally involved during his brief visit by the figure of an old man. There is something enigmatic about this man, aged yet strong, weighed down as if burdened with something more ponderous than the struggle for survival that faced all poor farmers in New England in the early nineteenth century. There seems to be a mystery that the narrator seeks to unravel, and the reader begins to share his quest. The narrator's growing determination to discover what the townsfolk do not seem at all eager to discuss bears fruit; an informant is willing to talk. We can now enter the home and meet the three persons who reside there. First we learn how they arrived at their permanent destination, and we discover the nature and depth of their suffering, even the cause of it, but we can never know why persons who stray so little from the accepted ways of the world must pay so dearly for their small transgressions.

The town in which the story unfolds is called Starkfield, in Massachusetts, and the name sets the tone for the characters, their lives, their surroundings. Geoffrey Walton writes that one "has a sense of a narrow world, whose foundations are religious, closing in on the inhabitants and of poverty, sickness, and inescapable unhappiness." In this novel, Walton contends, "the contrasts are a little too sharp, the setting a little too bleak, the characters almost caricature—of a grim kind, the disaster melodramatic, and the end unrelievedly wretched."[2]

This is the story of a young love that enters the dreary life of a man and ignites flames of which he was unaware—if he had ever felt them before, they were not within his powers of recall. The burden of his life does not consist only of the hard work of the New England farmer, struggling against difficult winters, the vicissitudes of climate, the endless effort to accumulate the dollar that will make the following year just a trifle easier. There is a wife, Zenobia (or Zeena, as she is also called), and if at rare moments one feels a flash of sympathy for her, it is not because she has earned it during the first seven years of their marriage (it is after seven years that the events leading to the tragedy occur); but perhaps she has not earned anything worse. Frome sometimes thought, Wharton writes, in a memorable passage whose economy of words all the more tellingly portrays the depth of feeling, that if it had not been winter when his mother died, he would never have married Zeena.

She was some distant cousin who had come to serve his mother as housekeeper, nurse, and companion, as the old lady went about the business of dying. It took many years for death to come, and by that time he was alone except for this woman in the house. Bleakness must have engulfed him. The death, even if he had been awaiting it, must have left him with that empty loneliness when suddenly there is nothing where once there had been movement, noise, complaints, a person, a warm body, even in its ailing form. He returns from the burial of his mother on a wintry day. One can feel the tough and biting winds, see the gray sky, and huddle in the cold too sad for an ordinary day but particularly for the day of a funeral. It is a time when the ground looks colder to the living than it feels to the dead. Thus Ethan comes back to his home, or what could be passing as home, alone with the woman who, with his dying mother and himself, had occupied the house. Where would she go, her task completed, her charge now dead? And he? The idea of a wife, even Zenobia, hardly an inspiration, was nothing more than the extension of the thought of avoiding complete reclusiveness. On a wintry afternoon, with early darkness setting in, it might have meant warmth to him. So they became man and wife.

We learn little of their marriage. It is childless, and it must have been nearly sexless, for she emerges as a character with little drive for sensual pleasure for herself and who must have been exceptionally successful in extinguishing what sexuality surged within him. Financial struggle follows them in this marriage, becoming aggravated with time and exacerbating an already difficult relationship. He is a youth still in his twenties, she is a sickly woman seven years his senior, complaining even as his mother had done, or worse, and falling more and more into a world of ailments, real and imagined. She is the hypochondriac who is really sick, with aches that are there, or when they are not she produces them and talks herself and others into believing in them. She turns to nostrums, quacks, faith healers, doctors she hears of here and there, spending the little money that they otherwise so frugally conserve on medicines and medicine men. She cannot assist him on the farm, she cannot take care of the home, she needs more than rest and drugs: she needs help, someone who will come and serve and scrub, to be her nurse and housemaid. It was not uncommon for the poor to have help of that sort; those who came to work were sort of indentured servants, literally without wages, while being trained for life as wife and home-maker. This was their education and apprenticeship. Sometimes it was a poor cousin or second cousin, less fortunate than oneself, who needed a home and who might have starved if she had not been taken in.

The entry of a girl into such a household must immediately create temptations. It is only after one has met Ethan and Zeena Frome that the initial utter sexlessness of such a trio can be imagined. Their lives are so devoid of passion, in any sense, that they cannot think in terms of marital disaster emanating from a third and younger person living side by side in the small house with the sickly and complaining wife and the virile, handsome, and hardworking younger husband. They take their fates for granted, in a spirit of complaint from her side, resignation from his; their fates are unfathomable and unwarranted, unearned and undeserved, but these are not people who look elsewhere. At least, not until the temptations have become greater than they can withstand.

Such is the sad, simple, and unendingly hopeless marriage of Zeena and Ethan Frome when Zeena's cousin, Mattie Silver, enters their lives. She does not come without blemish. Her father has somehow been involved in a scandal in which money was lost and perhaps handled unscrupulously, and upon Mattie has fallen poverty as well as disgrace. She is grateful for the home where she will be fed, or at least be allowed to prepare the food and feed herself, while she works for her keep and serves the apprenticeship that will enable her to enter, experienced yet virginal, upon a career as homemaker and housewife.

There are only slight signs that Ethan is taking note of Mattie as a woman, and the reader is left to speculate as to how conscious he is of his own growing interest. He takes to shaving every day. When he calls for her after a local dance, he is not pleased at the attention being paid her by the eligible young men of the neighborhood. But his own jealousy, his realization that he cannot lose her, that his fate is tied to hers, does not become fully and painfully evident to himself and Mattie until he is given the opportunity to spend a night alone with her in the isolated farmhouse, while Zeena goes off to a neighboring town to see yet another doctor. After his wife's departure, Ethan laughs as he has not laughed before, and discovers that there is joy and a gaiety within him while he thought they were dead. It is a jovial moment, and that it is made possible by the sufferings of his wife in no way burdens him. Only the brevity of the time that they will be allowed together serves to disturb the happiness and serenity of the experience.

They will celebrate. From a shelf they take a pickle dish that Zeena had received as a wedding gift from Aunt Philuria Maple and had carefully put away, as if in a museum, to be cherished, preserved, but not used. It is part of their defiance of Zeena and their momentary revelry. But the cat jumps on the table and knocks over the pickle dish which now appears before the couple as pieces of broken glass. Mattie is overcome by fear, immediately conjuring up the image of the mistress of the house, her gaunt face, her boundless anger, as she demands an explanation. But Ethan gives her strength. The next day he will obtain glue and put it together, carefully placing it where it had been, there to remain, to all appearances as if it had never been touched, probably for months or years before Zeena would notice that it was no longer whole and perfect. The moment of dampened mood passes, and after an evening of otherwise uneventful happiness she retires: goes to her room and closes the door, leaving him at the foot of the stairs. The old New England morality prevails, or at least the morality as Edith Wharton and many others believed it to have been.

The return of Zeena the next day is earlier than anticipated, and is preceded by a pitiable and desperate search for glue in the local store, an effort all the more frightening to Ethan because he is fearful of careless talk that will reach the ears of his wife. She returns to inform him that she is even more ill than she had imagined, and that she requires a full-time caretaker. But we cannot afford another person, Ethan protests, and Zeena makes the announcement, with the coldness that betrays for the first and only time her own suspicions that her husband's interests in Mattie have gone beyond her standards of respectability, that Mattie will go. In fact, the new househand will be coming the following day, and Mattie will leave at the same time. She will get her things ready, and without ceremony make her departure; one of the hired hands will take her to the station, and then he will go on to meet the newcomer.

Ethan is shaken, he argues and pleads, does all but threaten that he too will leave. That is beyond him. It is not so much that it is outside the scope of the moral choices that a man of the period, place, and social class can make. On the contrary, he has given it consideration, working out costs and figures with pencil and paper. It would require only fifty dollars for him to make the first step and escape to the west with Mattie, and it is not even the hardships that they would then face or the suffering of Zeena, abandoned and deserted, that deter him. It is simply impossible to place his hands on that sum of money. What little loyalty to Zeena and to the marriage vows that he has, and at that moment it is very little, is fortified by the economic argument: he cannot obtain the money to leave, and would not have the wherewithal to start again. He is entrapped and enchained. If money were available, he would buy his way out and the moral principles would be thrown to the wind. But in the end he discards such fantasies; the burdens and sacrifices that they would entail are both apparent and overwhelming. Instead, he faces the fact that Mattie is about to depart, and with her his last good hope of freedom from bondage to Zeena.

Ethan's arguments are in vain, his supplications to Zeena are rejected. It is as if she believes, or some suspicion of this belief has come upon her, not that there is infidelity in the sexual sense of the term, but that her husband is obtaining a slight pleasure from the presence of Mattie. That is enough to banish the girl from their home. Pleasures denied to herself, by illness real and unreal, by financial suffering, are not the entitlement of Ethan. If he has found even the briefest relief from the burden of life by her cousin's being in their home, that is itself reason that Mattie should not be there. It is not so much a cruel world that Wharton is painting, nor even a cruel woman in Zeena, but the stoic New England ascetic who, in the Calvinist tradition, lives by the principle that pleasure itself is evil, and that people are more likely to enter the kingdom of Heaven if they have denied themselves this-worldly gratifications. Denied to oneself, the pleasures hence cannot be allowed to others. It is a world that Wharton had never known, nor had her immediate forefathers, but she knew that it had existed and that her own class had benefited from its exploitation. Further, if their childlessness suggests, by the slightest implication, the sexlessness in which Zeena and Ethan must be engulfed, it represents even more how barren they are in every aspect of their lives, sexual and other, and she more than he.

She discovers the broken pickle dish and in her fury confronts the culprits who, in her absence, had quite obviously been frolicking in her house and touching her most precious belongings, while she was taking care of her mounting ailments and trying to survive newly discovered pains. What utter betrayal! It is this scene that is memorable in the minds of many readers, capturing as it does the anger that punctuates a world of gloom. "When I think of *Ethan Frome*," writes Louis Auchincloss, who places it among Wharton's best works, "I visualize a small painting, perfectly executed to the last detail, of three silent figures in a small dark cottage kitchen, with snow glimpsed through a window, the terrible Zeena in the center, white and pasty and gaunt, and, scattered on the table, the pieces of a broken dish."[3]

The decision that Mattie must go has already been made, and now it is just a matter of hours, to give her time to pack her things and hurriedly leave the house, carrying with her other meager belongings the contempt of the woman, her cousin, who had sheltered her and taught her.

Ethan Frome is a man of strength and of weakness, slightly exaggerated, perhaps, in both directions, precisely because these clashing and antithetical forces are present in all of us. In males, however, Wharton could depict the strength in firmer lines without implications of pathology, while showing their weaknesses as manifestations of human frailty more prominently than would be seen in women. Ethan's decision not to run off with Mattie is both: but it is weakness more than strength, for he is not held by the vows of loyalty that he had once taken and which had to be obeyed, come what may, nor by the ability to overcome the temptations that beckoned to him. Rather, it is that the new life that he saw, and that Mattie compels him to see, would be fraught with hardships and dangers.

In the moment of romantic temptation, he allowed Mattie to walk into her room without following her. One is almost tempted to say that he is not a romanticist, but it is more accurate to say that he is incapable of seizing an opportunity. He slips through life allowing choices to be made for him rather than making them for himself. But the shred of strength in Ethan can be found in the one symbolic stand that he takes, when he rises against Zeena and to her surprise insists—for Ethan is a crushed individual who seldom shows himself capable of insistence in confrontation with another—that he and he alone will take Mattie to the station and only then will he call for the new girl. Zeena urges him to stay and fix the furnace in the room that the girl will occupy and that Mattie is now leaving, but he replies that if the stove in its present condition was good enough for Mattie, it will have to do for the new one, too. He is unmovable. Feeble and shaken by the loss that he is facing, he is nonetheless strong as a mountain. Maybe Zeena has so completely won that she is willing to retreat; having stepped back, no matter how slightly, hers will still be the victory. She will be the lady of the miserable and poverty-stricken manor, when he returns that night with the girl that she has chosen to replace the one she has grown to resent. Or, perhaps, she may sense that her continued insistence is pushing him beyond the level of his tolerance. There is no love for the man, no loyalty, no interest in his welfare; but he is her caretaker, as he has vowed to be and as he will have to be for the few remaining years of her ailing life. There is the slim possibility that he would do the unthinkable: pushed too far, he might walk away from her entirely. It is a small concession she is making at the moment of her almost complete triumph.

So that the setting is made for the dénouement that will follow. Ethan and Mattie go to town together, with her packed trunk, prepared to say their farewells. He is almost ready to leave her, to relinquish the last bit of hope in life, and, equally ambivalent, she has resigned herself to the departure. Running away together is folly. They talk openly of their love and need for each other, and perhaps he wonders if he was not better off before a glimmer of hope had entered his life; whether the continued life with the joyless woman to whom he will return has not become more difficult now that he has met and lost Mattie. They have not even brought their love to fruition, never touched or embraced, but have only known that this was possible. He has seen in his dreams another life in another world, and cannot reach it; unable to reach it, he is likewise unable to return to the life that awaits him.

One experience of pure joy: they will take a ride on the sled down the hill. He sits behind her, holding the steering ropes, screams to her not to be scared, and when they reach bottom he asks her if she had thought that he was going to run into the elm. The question is innocent, but it plants the seeds of an idea that almost immediately comes before them:

> "I told you that I was never scared with you," she answered.
> The strange exaltation of his mood had brought on one of his rare fits of boastfulness. "It *is* a tricky place, though. The least swerve, and we'd never ha' come up again. But I can measure distances to a hair's breadth—always could."
> She murmured: "I always say you've got the surest eye . . ."
> Deep silence had fallen with the starless dusk, and they leaned on each other without speaking; but at every step of their climb Ethan said to himself: "It's the last time we'll ever walk together." (P. 163)

The words have a prophetic, almost macabre, yet unintended ambiguity that the man who was articulating them could not have fathomed. They say goodbye, but he insists that he cannot let her go, and she responds with equal ardor. There is nothing in front of them for as long as either can foresee the future. He tries to assure her that a good life awaits her, that she will find a man and marry him, and she tells him that she would almost rather be dead than married to another. Perhaps this, the first hint of an alternative, plants the idea of a second sleigh ride in her mind. Death is proposed as the way out, and the first suggestion of it comes from Mattie: "Ethan! Ethan! I want you to take me down again!" Where, he asks. Down the hill, she explains, down in the manner that he had said that they had barely escaped, only by the sureness of his hand, down so that they would neither of them ever come up again, exactly what he had barely finished saying had almost happened, or could have, had it not been for the steady hand. She pleads, he hesitates, lured both by his strength and weakness, and then orders her to the back of the sled. They have found the way out, and it is with impetuosity, with impulsiveness, almost with ecstasy, that they embrace it. They who cannot live together will die together, in a moment of joy, not unlike *l'amour fatal*. They will take the sled to the top of the hill, proceed down the most dangerous pathway, and it will gain momentum, they will be together as they fly over the snow with terrifying speed, he at the reins, steering straight for the tall, broad menacing elm that cannot but spell death for the riders.

He orders her to the back, and she inquires how he will be able to steer, sitting in front, and he replies only that he wants to feel her holding on to him. Does he also want to take the greater brunt of the collision, to be more certain that he will be the one killed if only one of them meets death?

They are on the path, they are flying toward the elm, it is waiting, growing ever larger in front of them, and it is he, not she, who wavers. Whatever fright overcomes her, whatever fleeting second thoughts she harbors, wishes that there were some way to undo what is about to be done, we do not know. The author abandons her, a pawn who does not have the steering gear in her hands and hence is both helpless and irrelevant to the outcome:

> The big tree loomed bigger and closer, and as they bore down on it he thought: "It's waiting for us: it seems to know." But suddenly his wife's face, with twisted monstrous lineaments, thrust itself between him and his goal, and he made an instinctive movement to brush it aside. The sled swerved in response, but he righted it again, kept it straight, and drove down on the black projecting mass. There was a last instant when the air shot past him like millions of fiery wires; and then . . . (P. 170)

There the passage ends, with the dots that tell us that the movement continues and that imply without description or explication the events that follow. From the accident he awakens to feel Mattie's face and to hear the sorrel whinny up the hill, then to lapse into unconsciousness. There is little left of the story. Their love has ended in a tragedy greater than death, and we are back with the narrator, for a few brief moments, now that he has learned why Ethan Frome, twenty-four years later, only fifty-two years of age, walks with stooped and heavy carriage as if there rested upon his shoulders the burdens that no man had ever known before.

They both survive, not only Ethan but Mattie, and the slight swerve of the sled, which came about when Zeena's face flashed so briefly in front of him, a painful image that he had sought immediately to banish, has left Mattie more victimized, at least physically, than Ethan.

In the years that have passed since the fateful ride toward the elm tree, the three principals in this tale of hardship have become locked in with one another. Instead of one person to whom Ethan is bound, there are two. From the most romantic moment of Ethan's life, to sacrifice his life in a suicide pact because the lovers could neither part nor have each other, there has emerged the most unromantic of triangles. Paralyzed, bound to a wheelchair, helpless and hard and bony, Mattie sits. Not a sign of the vivacity that had been part of her youth, nor of the verve with which she had once infused him, is apparent.

Complaining as much as before, with new troubles and pains as well as a continuity of the old ones, there is Zeena. But now Zeena is Mattie's servant, and as she serves her erstwhile maid, Zeena like Mattie must be looking at Ethan with untold resentment. The fates of each, their daily lives, are interwoven with the others, as the three live out their joyless days and years, in a home that is a prison, and to which they are not less bound because it has no guards or turrets, no watch-towers or bars. It is as if Wharton wanted to end her story with a line of irony, unwritten but surely present: "and they lived unhappily ever after."

Atonement is the theme of *Ethan Frome:* it is suffering and punishment endured because a person is paying his dues. And Ethan, Zeena, and Mattie are paying, they are paying and paying and paying, and their debt can never be paid. Only death will some day free them from their eternal hell, and each can hope that it comes first to him or her, not to the others; each will not want to be the survivor to face only one of the other, in the triad of hatred and resentment that is boundless.

Yet, in the end, exactly what is the nature of the evil, the sin, the crime, the transgression, call it what you will, for which they are atoning? Are they each a Christ on a crucifix, living (which is far worse than dying) for the sins of mankind? Hardly. They are not such majestic figures, they are less than noble, and in Wharton's worldview it is not for the sins of others that we suffer, but our own. This is no story of innocence and it is not one that offers hope for redemption. Unlike Lord Jim, Ethan neither seeks to be redeemed nor is he presented as deserving of it. Yet there is a similarity: like Jim, his was a moment of faltering, a lifetime of agony. Jim heard the word "Jump," and the next thing he knew, he was in the lifeboat; one never hears Marlow say that he jumped. The omission is deliberate. He found himself in the lifeboat—he did not take the initiative to place himself there. The construction of the passage (the passage in the literature, the passage of time, the passage through space) is studied. On outside forces that yelled the word to him, on mysterious lapses during which something happened to him—not during which time he performed an act—on all of these, responsibility is placed. But there is hope in Conrad's view, for man can be redeemed, for whatever act he commits. In Wharton's there is none. Man can only suffer, he can suffer life and await the liberation that comes with death.

Each of the three in this Greeklike tragedy has aided and contributed to the downfall of all three and to their interlocked fate. Yet Zeena least of all, one might think, at least from the contributory viewpoint. She was hardly a warm and loving wife, nor is she a warm and loving character, but she had spent her younger years looking after his mother, and she remained to look after him. It is difficult to imagine that she had intrigued and enticed him, this sexless creature who must already have been less than exciting to a man seven years her junior. Yes, she complained, but she did have pains, and did come to expect that it was her husband's duty to listen to these complaints and to be compassionate in her endless miseries. Is it her fate to be betrayed by her husband and the young cousin she has sheltered, just at the moment when she has gone to see if there are any palliatives to relieve her worsening condition? Is it to be her earned deserts to wait endlessly upon this girl in the wheelchair, this woman whose presence is a constant reminder of the broken pickle dish and of the stolen pleasures that were surreptitiously smuggled into the home while she was away?

But Zeena is hardly so innocent. Ailing and aging, she does show that she is bent on sharing her joylessness with Ethan. If she does not hate him, she resents him, and what she resents above all is that, in stoic and puritanical New England, he might be able to locate some pleasures in life, be they ever so slight. She is the antihedonist, not so much for herself, for her complaints and her pains do bring her pleasure, but for others, and particularly for Ethan. There is a streak in Zeena that goes beyond hypochondria and self-indulgence; it is meanness, and like a child with a mother, she is directing it against the only person present to receive it: her husband. Yes, she has her redemption and her meanness, too; they are one and the same interwoven into a single stream of life. She becomes the caretaker of the girl she had sent away, and in so doing, she becomes the constant reminder to her husband of the sin that he had committed in so much as entertaining a dream of abandoning her.

Mattie sits in the chair, she gives orders, she is crippled. Her beauty and youth have abandoned her. She had not entered this home as a girl in order to entice Ethan. In her innocence, she had served the couple well and had not sought to disrupt whatever bonds had held them together. She was the victim of a hating relationship which she could hardly have foreseen; and she had not intended her presence to give new depths of hatred and resentment to what was already smoldering there. When sent away, she was ready to go, except that at the very last moment, almost impulsively, certainly without internal conspiracy with her other selves, she suggests that there is a way out. She puts her full faith in Ethan, and holding tightly the man she loves, the man whose strength permits her to hold with confidence, she goes almost in joyous ecstasy to their doom. Like lovers before and since, they will be united forever in their graves. She is certainly guiltless that her plot took an ironic twist: yes, united forever, but in life, not death, and more painfully in life than ever in death.

Mattie, sitting in her chair, will look forever at the man whose moment of weakness has transformed her into a lifelong cripple. Her faith must have been misplaced, and his courage had turned to cowardice in the end, at the moment when they were approaching the elm. It was a cowardice that saved his life but that cost her, not her life, for she had been ready and in fact determined to relinquish it, but the soundness of her body. His towering strength had been a well of weakness, and she its victim. If there is irony in her being served by Zeena, there can only be resentment every time Ethan opens the door, or looks up from the meal he is eating, and she sees the man whom she had been willing to die for, not to live for.

What of Ethan? Edmund Wilson was describing both Ethan Frome and other characters created by the same novelist when he wrote: "The typical masculine figure in Edith Wharton's fiction is a man set apart from his neighbors by education, intellect, and feeling, but lacking the force or the courage either to impose himself or to get away."[4] It is an accurate summary, as one would expect of the dean of American literary critics, but of Ethan one can go further. Set apart from the others in Starkfield, he made a feeble attempt, half-hearted, entirely botched, torn with ambiguity, and in the end suffered more from the effort to get away than he would have had he completely lacked the force and courage of which Wilson speaks.

For Ethan Frome, it was not merely weakness, that indetermination flashing down upon him, that had resulted in the greater tragedy replacing the one that had been planned and expected. It might be interpreted as an iota of compassion: the face of Zeena coming before him, her suffering, her being abandoned by him, his obligations to her, real or assumed. It was Zeena who would be notified of her widowhood within hours, who would be left ailing and penniless, the poor, suffering, and sickly woman who had cared for his mother and then stayed on to care for him. He tries to banish this thought from his mind, but it is the entry of it, for that split millisecond in which some fates are determined, that saves his life and condemns him to a lifelong living hell, one from which escape will be possible only when death, in its natural and due course, with unhurried pace, comes to fetch him.

Yet such an interpretation is too simple for Wharton's penetrating study into the human psyche, and it may be too kind to Ethan to impute to him a compassion that he did not feel. Yes, the face of Zeena came flashing in front of him during the fateful (but not quite fatal) sleigh ride, but is this not Eros standing up in fear against Thanatos? Is this not the dread of death, the eleventh-hour or even later second thoughts about suicide, the wish to live and to save oneself that brings this torn and drawn face before the mind's eye? It is the call for help that, some would say, all suicides are indulging in, the call that so often results in the unsuccessful attempt. There is nothing to suggest that it was pure compassion that brings her to his mind and that causes the swerving of the sled, nor on the contrary that it is the unconscious drive to save himself, forcing itself into his consciousness. It is surely both; and being both, one's judgment of Ethan is tempered. His fate is undeserved, as any fate of such magnitude must be; but he is even less guiltless, there is even less to mitigate and extenuate him, than one might have expected.

True, he had not betrayed Zeena, at least not in the narrow sense in which that term is generally interpreted, an act that would have had an enormity at that time and in his social class position that it never had in the world of Wharton's peers. There was no way out from his loveless dreariness, except the ultraromantic plunge toward death with Mattie. Something had gone wrong, at that moment and in all of life, and now even the slight hope that an exit would be found, a relief short of years of suffering, has been snuffed out, the last flickering light is gone, and his world is dark and doomed.

Life is suffering, but for what misdeeds? For the fate of having become entwined with the wrong people, at the wrong time? For daring to plan to put an end to that suffering, taking from God or the fates the right to decide when life shall be over? For wavering from one's set path and allowing duty and obligation and the memory of the sufferings of others, or of anticipated and forthcoming hurts and harms, to intervene? For being weak when the world demands strength? For hesitation that, unplanned and unwanted, saves oneself, only to bring greater injury to another? For being strong when weakness itself—as Zeena has so forcefully demonstrated, and then as Mattie in her crippled years will, as well—is the most powerful strength?

In the world of religion, suffering is handled through atonement.

We are not Christs, we are not suffering for the sins of others but of ourselves, and we will not rise from the dead nor will we have a second chance, a second coming. We are enemies of ourselves and of all with whom we become intertwined, and we can avoid suffering by avoiding alliances. But we cannot, for in so doing we would be avoiding the loves that alone can alleviate the sufferings.

It is interesting that in Judaism and in Christianity, so dissimilar although they have a common origin, the former sets aside as its holiest period the day of atonement, the latter the day of the birth of the Son of God. Atonement is a cleansing, an admission of our evils and a denial of body pleasure in order to be forgiven and then become at one with the deity again. The suffering is time-limited, and when darkness descends at sundown, announcing that the day is ended, the sacrifice and denial can come to an end, too. For Ethan Frome and the two women, it is atonement without hope of forgiveness. The darkness that will descend to relieve them will not mark the end of the day but of life.

We are caught, all of us, in Wharton's world, and her story is powerful because it is both the unique tragedy of three persons and the universal history of mankind. The narrator is humanity, observer of oneself; he seeks to discover what has happened to his fellow man whom he observes to be overburdened, aged, and lined. What he discovers is a tragedy that the sufferers do not comprehend.

Inevitability and inertia mark the lives in this story; theirs is a pathetic helplessness of persons caught up in what they see as destiny. They rise to no moral heights, perhaps because they do not accept responsibility for having fashioned their own fate. It is all something that has happened to them.

Alfred Kazin writes that Wharton specialized in tales of victimization.[5] Certainly *Ethan Frome* fits this description, for all three characters are victims, but they appear to be victims more of some inevitable and inexorable fate than of one another, or of themselves. It is easy to imagine that, if blaming comes to their minds during the years of anguish and pain that follow the accident, Zeena is placing the responsibility on Ethan and Mattie, and how she might divide it one can hardly conjecture; Mattie on Zeena and Ethan, perhaps the latter having the greater share; and Ethan on Zeena, but not without recalling that the suggestion for the suicide pact that led to the tragedy came from Mattie.

One wonders if any of the three persons who inhabit Wharton's novel might be capable of believing that he or she has fashioned circumstances and has made life what it is, for himself and the two others. For although in the suicide scene Ethan shows himself to be a romantic in the same sense that this is displayed by Lord Jim as he goes to his death, Jim had made an effort to take responsibility, had told Jewel that he

was not good enough for the world out there, and had sought to retrieve his lost honor, not just to bear the suffering of its loss. With
Ethan there is only the pain, remorse, not in the sense of repentance,
but in the fantasy of how much better things would have been had they
been different. There is no indication that Ethan finally accepts the fact
that it was he who had chosen to embark on the path that led to the
fate that befell him. It is thus not only moral decisions that the characters in this novel avoid making, as Lionel Trilling so astutely reminds
us, it is decision itself.[6] Things happen to Ethan, he does not make them
happen, and this is true from the moment of the marriage until the
image of Zeena comes into his mind and "the sled swerved."

Irving Howe could well have been speaking of Ethan Frome as
much as any of the other works of Wharton when he writes that the
texture of her novels is dark. "Like so many writers whose education
occurred during the latter decades of the nineteenth century, she felt
that the universe—which for her is virtually to say, organized society—
was profoundly inhospitable to human need and desire."[7] He then proceeds to quote a passage from one of Wharton's works, *The Fruit of the
Tree*. "Life is not a matter of abstract principles, but a succession of
pitiful compromises with fate, of concessions to old traditions, old beliefs, old tragedies, old failures." Commenting, Howe adds: "This sense
of fatality has, in her best work, a certain minor magnificence, what
might be called the magnificence of the bleak."[8]

Bleakness certainly envelops the little house in Starkfield where
Mattie, Zeena, and Ethan are quartered many years after the accident.
It is a bleakness that shows no promise of coming to an end, and there
was not even a pitiful compromise with fate, but only an abject surrender to it.

Mattie has been cheated of the death she had asked of Ethan, and
indeed, as the narrator is told by one of the townspeople, a Mrs. Hale,
it was a pity that she did live. Of course it is a pity. Death is atonement
which puts an end to suffering. Sundown cannot come so quickly for
Mattie, or for the others. After her death (had she died), Ethan would
have cried, repented, apologized, explained, perhaps lied or confessed
or made some combination of the two, and then, little by little, would
have cleansed himself of the memories even as he had been cleansed of
the bruises that he suffered. In her death, he could have found an
occasional respite from guilt. Body and soul would have healed together, neither to return quite to the point where they had been before
(nothing ever does), but both to continue, perhaps the better for the
experience. But Wharton is too acerbic in her view of humanity to
permit such a relatively pleasant solution to the problems that face these
people. They are doomed to live:

Mrs. Hale paused a moment, and I remained silent, plunged in the vision of what her words evoked. "It's horrible for them all," I murmured.
"Yes: it's pretty bad. And they ain't any of 'em easy people either. Mattie *was*, before the accident; I never knew a sweeter nature. But she's suffered too much—that's what I always say when folks tell me how she's soured. And Zeena, she was always cranky. Not but what she bears with Mattie wonderful—I've seen that myself. But sometimes the two of them get going at each other, and then Ethan's face'd break your heart . . . When I see that, I think it's *him* that suffers most . . . anyhow it ain't Zeena, because she ain't got the time . . . It's a pity, though," Mrs. Hale ended, sighing, "that they're all shut up there'n that one kitchen. In the summertime, on pleasant days, they move Mattie into the parlour, or out in the door-yard, and that makes it easier . . . but winters there's the fires to be thought of; and there ain't a dime to spare up at the Fromes'." (Pp. 179–180)

Then Mrs. Hale ends by saying that if Mattie had died the week after the accident, Ethan might have lived; this way, there's not much difference between the Fromes up at the farm and those down at the graveyard.

This is not the view of the narrator, nor of the author, but rather of the woman who tells him the story. There is a great difference. Mattie did not die, because no one is entitled to such an easy way out. But sufferings do not last forever. "While there's death, there's hope," wrote the British critic and biographer James Pope-Hennessey. It might have been an epigraph for Wharton's novel, and an epitaph for Frome's tombstone.

Until then, our destiny is not only to face tomorrow, but to face in our tomorrows the wrongs and misdeeds, the errors and miscalculations that we committed yesterday. Edith Wharton knew this, as few other authors have; and she gave us in Ethan Frome the man who will epitomize it for all of us.

NOTES

1. Alfred Kazin, *On Native Grounds* (New York: Harcourt, Brace & World, 1942), p. 81.

2. Geoffrey Walton, *Edith Wharton: A Critical Interpretation* (Rutherford, N.J.: Fairleigh Dickinson University Press, 1970), pp. 79, 82.

3. Louis Auchincloss, *Edith Wharton* (Minneapolis: University of Minnesota Press, Pamphlets on American Writers, No. 12, 1961), p. 21.

4. Edmund Wilson, "Justice to Edith Wharton," in Irving Howe, ed., *Edith Wharton: A Collection of Critical Essays* (Englewood Cliffs, N.J.: Prentice-Hall, 1965), pp. 26–27; taken from Wilson, *The Wound and the Bow* (New York: Oxford University Press, 1947).

5. Kazin, *On Native Grounds*, p. 77.

6. Lionel Trilling, "The Morality of Inertia," in Howe, ed., *Wharton: A Collection;* originally published in Robert MacIver, ed., *Great Moral Dilemmas* (New York: Harper, 1956).

7. Irving Howe, *A World More Attractive* (New York: Horizon, 1963), p. 55.

8. Ibid., p. 58.

7

TEMPLE DRAKE
The Failure of Redemption, the Triumph of Faith

In the life work of William Faulkner there is a *comédie humaine,* but it is limited geographically and even circumscribed somewhat by time. The world that he is depicting is the old American South, declining, decaying, disintegrating under his eyes, the South that had almost disappeared, or had lost at least its outer façades, its presentation of self to the rest of humanity, before Faulkner's own portrait of it was completed. Although his Nobel Laureate speech expressed confidence in the endurance, the survival, and the triumph of humanity, his writings give only the slightest glimpse of his conviction of such an eventuality, or even that he recognized the germ of it residing somewhere within the society around him. It was not a revolution that he saw, in which the new would replace the rotting and rotten corpse of the old, which, dying or perhaps dead, is still clung to with ardor, embraced with faith that is so often confused with hope, for without such faith there would be only a vacuum. Faulkner's powerful short story "A Rose for Emily," while on one level a macabre tale of love and even necrophilia, on another summarizes the writer's vision of all human relations.

No Gothic writer, no picaresque novelist leading a protagonist from one haunt of decadence to another, could have compiled so thor-

All quotations from *Sanctuary* and *Requiem for a Nun* are from the Vintage paperback editions (New York, n.d., for *Sanctuary,* and New York, 1975, for *Requiem*).

ough and, to many readers, so repellent a "laundry list" of degradations as are found in Faulkner. Incest, illegitimacy, adultery, the already mentioned hint of necrophilia, imbecility, race hatred in the raw from the old rednecks, race hatred in its subtler but perhaps more insidious form as expressed by the white aristocracy, whoredom, rape: they are all there, and many more, each in a manifestation seldom equalled, certainly not surpassed, by his contemporaries. Nothing is made pretty except the prose, the brilliant turns of phrase which stand out in bold relief against the ugliness and sordidness of the persons and activities they depict. Glittering words shine all the brighter in contrast with a content of somber shadows. In a manner encountered both in works of art, for effects not otherwise obtainable, and in pornographic and other commercial productions designed solely for exploitation of a market, Faulkner appears to search with studied deliberation for mechanisms to jolt, disturb, shock, and sometimes disgust the reader. In so doing, he is merciless toward his own South and particularly the state of Mississippi, which he loved and in which he had sunk roots; and if the Mississippians claimed him as their own, this is the fate of genius. Unlike Joyce, who was banned from Eire during his life, anathema to the Church, only to become a showpiece of pride when he could no longer use his mighty pen against them, Faulkner was the darling of the South whose depths of degradation he understood even while he was satirizing and flagellating the people who were lionizing him. Perhaps they did not understand the nature of his message, or even its content; certainly, the Southern aristocrats did not believe that a great part of their constituency could understand his work or would be capable of reading it. In that there is an irony, from which a reader of Faulkner never escapes and which one constantly appreciates, for the ignorance that he portrayed as a central theme throughout his work never prevented those he depicted from becoming his admirers.

In his study of violence in the American novel, W. M. Frohock sees Faulkner as writing not about Southerners but about all humanity: "to be surrounded by evil, and inevitably, out of their own natures, to be both victims and workers of evil"—such is their fate, such is the vision of Faulkner.[1]

It was a world of corruption that he saw, but was it not also a world of redemption? If so, is there not an ambivalence here that justifies a more hopeful view of humanity? The key figure in Faulkner's depiction of redemption is no doubt Temple Drake, central character of *Sanctuary* and, together with Nancy, of its sequel, *Requiem for a Nun*, written some twenty years later but taking place only eight years after the events of the earlier work. But Temple Drake, upon analysis, turns out to be a redeemed figure manquée, a failure not only because the goal she seeks—which brings her to the confession that for her appears to be an expiation, or at least a partial one—is always unattained, but also because her confession contains a major flaw that introduces distortion. In the language of criminal justice it is the truth that she tells, however reluctantly, but not the whole truth, and in philosophical terms, this is a contradiction for less than the whole truth is not the truth.

There are two themes here: the aim of the confession, which at least on its manifest level is not achieved; and the content of the confession, with its misplaced emphasis. These are interwoven, but only in the most implicit manner. The failure of Temple's confession derives from its basic dishonesty, with its omission, significant but never explicit, leaving many critics and readers at odds over the message of the author.

For the early 1930s, when Faulkner wrote *Sanctuary*, the violence in the novel could hardly have been stronger. It is not enough that the central scene is a rape: it must be committed by an impotent and cruel criminal, Popeye, a moonshiner, racketeer, and murderer who, to effect the assault on Temple, resorts to the use of an instrument, a corn-cob, to replace his own inadequate anatomy. When he becomes aware that he is being watched by Tommy, a well-meaning and slow-witted man who has sought to protect Temple, Popeye makes certain that Tommy can no longer serve as a threat to him in the one way that such certainty can be obtained: he kills him.

Popeye brings Temple to Memphis and makes her a prisoner in a whorehouse, but he is still faced with the dilemma of how he is to enjoy the woman whom he has in his own brutal manner possessed. He obtains Red, who is young, strong, handsome, virile, and evidently quite skillful in the art of copulation, and while Popeye watches at the bedside, drooling, trembling with passion fulfilled yet unfulfilled, Red and Temple lie on the bed and, in the phrase of a later generation, make out. If ever the cliché "a vicarious thrill" were justified, almost to the point where it dilutes the meaning of an event, it is in this scene.

There is a striking similarity here to Lady Chatterley's affairs, first with the novelist but much more with the gardener; yet there are too many differences to allow the analogy to go unchallenged. There is impotence on the part of both males who lay claim to the woman, but for Lawrence it is the impotence of the entire British upper class, while for Faulkner it is the decay of the ruthless and ignorant whites, upper and lower, who had ruled the South unchallenged for decades. In Lawrence, Lord Chatterley accepts with anguish and resignation the fact that he is paralyzed and impotent, very much as does the House of Lords, with the propriety and good manners that the British show among themselves (but never to colonial peoples). In Faulkner, the brutality and desperation of the impotent are dramatized so that the substitute phallus and later the spectator role are symbols of an unwillingness to surrender to biological fate and to accept that one cannot have what one cannot have. Faulkner's is a society of dissolute people, and the dissolute by extension inhabit a world in dissolution; in Lawrence, there is a new world of vigor and strength being born out of the decay of the old.

In both novels, *Sanctuary* and *Lady Chatterley's Lover,* the woman turns to another for the fulfillment she cannot obtain from the man who claims proprietary rights to her, in one instance by possession, and in the other by marriage. Constance Chatterley is Lady Chatterley, in the title of the book and in every act, and if she were not a woman of the aristocracy the work would lose much of its meaning. The passionate, sensuous, immoral, and promiscuous woman of *Sanctuary* also has an interesting name: Temple. She is Southern white woman idolized in a sort of secular Maryolatry, placed before the world as asexual, frigid, and hence pure; and in that sense she is Faulkner's counterpart of Joyce's Penelope, who during the wanderings of her Ulysses stayed home and accepted every suitor. Further, if Temple's name has a significance, so has Popeye's. His surname is Vitelli: the man who, with Lord Chatterley, is the best-publicized impotent in literature, is named for life itself. A more devastating vision of the Southern white concept of vitality can hardly be imagined.

The two women are both upper-class whites whose purity has been defiled and who embrace a new sensuality. In so doing each betrays her social class, but in entirely different ways. Constance Chatterley does so as a free choice and an act of liberation, all of her own volition, and her betrayal exists only in the view of the peers she is abandoning. Temple Drake suffers with guilt. She is a prisoner in a double meaning, not only because she is being held by Popeye in the Memphis brothel, but because she cannot free herself of the passions that cause upheaval within her, yet she cannot control or accept them, either. When Constance goes to Lord Chatterley and tells him that she will seek a divorce, disclosing at the same time the name of the man with whom she will form a new life, she is renouncing the impotence of the British aristocracy for the lifeblood of the British working class. If this is romantic on the one hand, it is political on the other. She has no guilt, and hence no need for redemption. Lawrence's characters will survive, because Eros conquers over Thanatos.

Two subplots develop in *Sanctuary* that lay the basis both for the outcome of the novel itself and for the theme of its sequel (probably not planned at the time of the writing of *Sanctuary,* but all of Faulkner's works are so interwoven with a single place, entire groups of families and acquaintances, the Snopeses and the Sartorises and others, that one cannot say with confidence that *Requiem for a Nun* was completely unplanned when *Sanctuary* appeared). The first of the plots involves the death of Tommy, who was killed by Popeye. Lee Goodwin is arrested for the murder. A lower-class white, a bootlegger or moonshiner who lives on the farm where the murder was committed, he is a witness to the activities that have taken place there. He is a man with a prison record, a shabby and seamy life history, and who now has a family—a devoted woman with whom he is living as man and wife, and their baby. Horace Benbow, an upper-class lawyer who is convinced of Lee's innocence (and who had also been at the scene of the crime and met Lee and the others sometime before Temple's arrival), takes on the case and insists on defending the man, despite the hostility of Benbow's family as well as the townspeople (the South had not yet taken to the idea that people are entitled to counsel in a criminal trial), and the apparent hostility and generally peculiar attitude of the defendant himself, who seems reluctant to cooperate in his own defense.

The second theme: back in Memphis, the prisoner in the sanctuary escapes for a few minutes to telephone Red, the surrogate copulator, and then voluntarily returns to her hideout. She has been sending him passionate letters and arranging for her escape, not back to her family and the protection of the law, but away from Popeye so that she and Red can pursue their lives of sexuality and sensuality. The plans go awry, and Popeye now commits his second murder (there may be others but they are not known and are not germane to the story) when he kills Red.

Horace Benbow discovers that Temple is living in the whorehouse in Memphis and manages to talk to her while Popeye is away and she is under the watchful eye of the madam of the brothel. By the time he leaves, he is certain that he will win the case by having her testify that it was not Lee but Popeye who killed Tommy. One can here speculate as to why Popeye found it necessary to murder Tommy. Was it because he did not want to be watched, that he had warned Tommy against "spying," and in his callous manner felt justified in disposing of him for ignoring these warnings? Was it because Tommy could have been a witness if Temple were to seek his arrest for the assault, and this act would dispose of the only person who could corroborate her story? Or was it because his own impotence, the lack of masculinity, would be exposed before another person, one other than the victim, and Popeye could not survive with that secret shared (although later he shares it by bringing Red to the bed, but this was to fulfill needs within him that were otherwise blocked)? All three explanations are possible, they can be synthesized, and yet all have their flaws. A Freudian interpretation is not at all far-fetched: unable to perform with a penis, Popeye at that moment takes hold of a hard, inflexible, and deadly instrument, symbolic of ejaculation, and discharges it in a display of manly power.

Popeye's reputation for proficiency and accuracy with a gun is almost mythic; it is in stark contrast with how little he can do with his penis. Lee fears him, fears especially the gun, and Temple does too, although her tie to her assaulter and oppressor goes far beyond fear. Even in jail, Lee is not free from the fear that, should he name the killer, he will be Popeye's next victim, whether a bullet reaches him while still in the protective custody of the jail or after his release; and although he does not specifically say so, he must be fearing for the lives of his woman and child as well. Thus, Lee resists any effort to help Horace Benbow win the case, refusing to name the murderer although asserting his own innocence. It is a lost cause, except for the success of Benbow in convincing Temple to testify.

Thus she is called to the witness stand, and as she testifies she cranes her neck to fix her eyes on someone or something in the rear of the courtroom. The object of her stare is not identified, and while at times she seems to be looking at Popeye, it is more likely her father and four brothers sitting there. Spellbound, fascinated, frightened, she testifies, telling a series of lies, betraying Horace, who had found her in the Memphis sanctuary, betraying Lee Goodwin and his wife, who had befriended her, and pointing to the defendant as both rapist and murderer. In fact, the story she narrates is essentially accurate, except that the names have been changed; instead of Popeye, it is Lee who has violated her and killed Tommy.

Faulkner is not yet finished with Southern justice. There is a nice little fire after the defendant has been found guilty (the jury takes eight minutes to reach its unanimous decision), and the courthouse jail is burned that night by a happy mob. "I wouldna used no corn-cob," one of the rednecks in the lynch group remarks, followed by a background chorus of salacious laughter. Temple has slipped out of the court with her father and her four brothers (we next meet her, in the last episode of the book, in the Luxembourg Gardens in Paris, talking to her father). Popeye leaves town, and on the road he is picked up for the murder of a policeman that had taken place sometime back in a small Southern town "at an hour when he was in another town killing somebody else." He is tried and found guilty—like the jury that convicted Goodwin, this one also takes eight minutes to reach its verdict. He too goes to his death; he who had killed two men and assisted in framing a third man for one of these murders is now himself railroaded to the gallows for a crime of which he has no knowledge, which occurred in a town where he had never before been, and at a time when he was far away committing another murder altogether. It is a neat little package of ironies, justice will out, and no one really cares about the niceties of guilt or innocence, constitutional rights, and the like, as long as worthless people are put out of the way.

As a commentary on Southern justice, *Sanctuary* is so flawed as hardly to be worth serious consideration; its only value is that it is a strong indictment, with innocent men being convicted, others not at all innocent being found guilty of crimes that they have not committed, and lawless gangs becoming impatient in awaiting the gallows or the intricacies and delays of appeals and making a party of an execution, robbing the hangman of his fee. Beyond this, even given the nature of the jurisprudential system in small towns in eastern Tennessee and the heart of Mississippi in the 1920s, there is much that is unconvincing about the cases themselves, particularly the trial of Lee. Temple comes to the stand apparently as a witness for the defense, and she immediately turns the tables and testifies against the defendant, substantiating the accusations that are already in the indictment, and adding evidence, motive, and other detail. Yet, there is not even an effort on the part of Horace to have her declared a hostile witness, so that he can impeach her testimony. Perhaps such legal maneuvers would have been of little use in the heart of Mississippi in 1928. After Temple has given the damaging testimony that will assure beyond doubt the verdict of guilt, she is again turned over to the defense for redirect examination, and Horace, discouraged, does nothing more than rest his case. He never confronts her with the glaring inconsistencies, does not establish that it is not his client who is impotent (the wife and child are in court), does not question Temple as to her whereabouts during the past several weeks, seeks to elicit neither the facts of her imprisonment nor the name of her abductor, and makes no inquiry as to why she is now telling a story completely at variance with what she had said during his talk with her in the Memphis sanctuary. The credibility of Temple as a witness could so easily have been impeached, the ability of a dedicated lawyer to demolish her is so apparent, that Horace Benbow emerges more as symbol than lawyer. He is a symbol of the discouragement, even demoralization, of those elements in the white South who would raise moral issues in a spirit of righteousness and indignation. He knows what the verdict will be, and he just walks away in complete dejection. Hardly the act of an officer of the court in a struggle for the life of a man, particularly one of whose innocence he is convinced and whose wife and child he has protected.

Approximately twenty years after *Sanctuary,* Faulkner published *Requiem for a Nun.* In the interim he had gained fame. From an unknown with a faithful following, mainly from his remarkable but not commercially successful novel *The Sound and the Fury,* which had earned him a small circle of enthusiasts, he had become a man showered with accolades by critics, many of whom considered him America's leading novelist (only Hemingway offered some competition in the eyes of several critics), possessing a wide world of admirers among men and women of letters and recognition as an accomplished master of style. Almost simultaneously with the publication of *Requiem* he became a Nobel Laureate in literature.

As a sequel to the earlier novel, *Requiem* picks up several of the main characters, particularly Temple, and follows their lives in the years after the events of *Sanctuary.* To a limited extent, this is a technique that Faulkner utilized quite frequently in novels that were not sequels to others but in which persons appear whom readers have known elsewhere; in an epilogue written for *The Sound and the Fury* many years after its publication, Faulkner tells us who did what after the last scene, when Quentin disappears with some money and slides down the drainpipe, slipping away from home, uncle, grandmother, and others. In *Requiem,* however, there is more than a lapse of time since the rape, abduction, and trial: there are the unresolved issues of Temple's life, as depicted in *Sanctuary,* now coming to the fore again. If *Sanctuary* is the story of the fall of a woman, *Requiem* is the story of her effort to rise. In this she fails.

Like Lord Jim after the inquiry, Temple Drake is in flight when we encounter her in *Requiem.* Again like Jim, she lives with a buried past, yet it is incompletely interred, for many of the facts are known not only to herself but to a few others around her. Further, there is no indication that she is a woman whose conscience is so strong that she lives in a constant ambience of inner guilt. About a year after the trial, she was married to the man whose drunken driving had been responsible in the first instance for her being stranded with Lee, Popeye, Tommy, and the other unfortunates. Temple has had two children with this man. One of them, the infant daughter, has been killed, and a black woman, Nancy (the "mammy" stereotype of the old South, or more exactly a combination of the bad black and the good mammy, carrying the stigma not only of race but of a promiscuous alcoholic, a dope fiend and prostitute) is awaiting execution for the murder of the infant. Almost in ecstasy, Nancy turns her cell into a joyous retreat; it is her sanctuary in which she sings gospel songs to God her Maker, to Whom she is about to return. Not only is there no sign of remorse or regret for what she has done, but no sorrow. She faces her future, and she is certain that there is a future for her, without fear. She can look back with a sense of self-satisfaction at her act, although to the townspeople and the public, who know nothing of her motive, it was cruel and senseless, as befits their image of a crime committed by a black whore and dope fiend, who was alcoholic to boot.

Nancy will die on the gallows, the date has been set, and while waiting for that to become a thing of the past, irrevocable, unchangeable, Temple has fled with her son, the older, survivor of the two children. They are in California, running like Lord Jim, away from people they know and who know them, until the child, with the startling and perceptive innocence that sometimes comes from a child because he has not yet learned the etiquette of silence, asks where they are going to run after March 13. Almost on the eve of the execution Temple receives a telegram to come home. It comes from her husband's uncle, who is serving without fee for the condemned woman (the few odd glimpses of heroics in Faulkner appear mostly to be centered on lawyers who are never successful in their efforts, while the rare events of heroism and self-sacrifice are committed only by the wretched, as if to say that it is only in apparent vice that one can discover virtue, or in the putatively vicious that one can find the genuinely virtuous).

The return of Temple sets the opening of the book, and stylistically it is from that point on an unusual work, actually two books interwoven, one more than the other the sequel to *Sanctuary*. Faulkner uses *Requiem* to tell the history of Yoknapatawpha County and the towns therein, particularly Jefferson, from the time of the first settlers, placing special attention on the courthouse and the jail, on a lock that was purchased, dragged, transported: it is as if Faulkner is both summarizing and recapitulating that sector of Southern history that involved him and his people (those around him and those created by him), and at the same time is stating that the history of the settlements, the first relationships with the Indians, the frontier events, and on and on were all nothing more than a series of incidents, one following upon another, all designed to culminate in the execution of a virtuous woman for a heroic act of self-sacrifice. Then, interspersed with these descriptive historical accounts—as convoluted as history itself with their asides, parenthetical remarks, and parens within parens, all as scintillating as they are annoying and informative—there is the setting itself.

The setting. There are four people on the scene and one in the background. The latter is Nancy; the others are Temple, her husband, her uncle by marriage, and the governor of Mississippi. The ease with which Temple Drake—she is now Temple Stevens, but the ghost of Temple Drake follows her and it is the Temple Drake surviving in Temple Stevens with which she must cope—and the uncle, a lawyer, are able to gain access to the governor in the middle of the night is not meant to highlight the urgency with which the situation is perceived, for the forthcoming execution of just another black murderess would certainly not be enough to awaken the governor for a conference at that hour. It is meant to be symbolic of the upper- and ruling-class milieu of the Old South from which Temple came and of which she remains a part. These scenes, the confrontations and dialogues, and the flashbacks to the night of the murder of the baby in which other characters make their appearance, are written in the form of a three-act play. It is a world and a war where action is verbal, a war of the words, in which persuasiveness alone can be triumphant. Acts themselves, other than verbal ones, are only to be talked about, or committed by lower-class persons and the fallen ones of the upper strata. In *Sanctuary* all is violence; in *Requiem* all is reminiscence, quietude, argument not with fists (much less corn-cobs or pistols) but with entreaties. Even the murder is offstage and is reported rather than committed in full view of an audience.

Temple has returned from her flight to plead for mercy for the woman who has murdered her six-month-old daughter, who has confessed to that crime but has not said a word about the temptation that brought her to it. Nancy Mannigoe is the epitome of virtue, and her greatest attribute, symbol of her altruism, for which she has come close to her God and is ready to be sanctified, is that the same reason that impelled her to murder the child, knowing that she would pay with her life, now compels her to remain silent about the events leading up to the crime. If Nancy goes to the gallows, she will be at least the fifth person in Temple's brief life for whose death she, Temple, will be responsible. For the first, Tommy's death at the hands of Popeye, she might have escaped culpability but by her exculpation of Popeye she has become an accomplice to the act. She had been the victim of Popeye, as much as Tommy albeit in a different way, but after the fact she acquiesced in the victimization. The second victim was Red: she had not trapped him, she had not wished to set him up, but it was her passion for him that caused him to fall from a bullet in an alleyway. Lee, the third, was an innocent man whom she could have saved (Faulkner does not make it clear, but perhaps there were two others, Lee's wife and child, and perhaps even others who happened to be unfortunate inhabitants of cells when Lee and the jailhouse burned to the ground). Her fourth victim was her own daughter, not because she herself had suffocated the infant—that had indeed been committed by Nancy—but because Nancy had done this to save Temple and the rest of the family from destruction and ruination. And now when the fifth, Nancy herself, was to go to her death, Temple had fled, refusing to give even the mitigating evidence that might have enabled a judge and a jury to see that this was not the woman responsible, in a moral sense, for the murder of the child.

The scenes that follow, except for flashbacks, are confessions on Temple's part to her uncle the lawyer, some in the presence of her husband (more exactly, he is hiding out of sight but not out of hearing range, and she does not know that he is listening until this is revealed after all the confessions are made), and to the governor, in her entreaties to commute the death sentence if not entirely pardon the convicted woman. These confessions form the bulk of the story, and it is in them that one searches for some evidence of redemption.

First in confrontations with the attorney, and then in the governor's office in the early hours of the morning, Temple does not pour out but is forced by persuasion, suggestion, and entreaty to tell her story. Actually, there are two stories that she must explain, the immediate past that led up to the slaying of the child, and the past past, the past that occurred before the past. The old past had been buried, Temple thought, forever. She was able to raise her head high in town because having been victim (to their knowledge) and not accomplice, she was able once again to be the respected and pure white woman. Even the defiling of her had not been so bad, for had it not occurred at the hands of a white man (or a white half-man)? It is not an easy story for her to narrate, for she is ridden with guilt. Hers is not a story of innocence trampled upon by the forces of evil, for she became the accomplice of evil, and it challenges the imagination to conceive of her as having offered strong resistance to the first tempters.

But the past returns. Talking to the governor about Temple, in her presence, describing her at the moment when the first child was on the way to being born, Uncle Stevens says:

> It was as though she realized for the first time that you—everyone—must, or anyway may have to, pay for your past; that past is something like a promissory note with a trick clause in it which, as long as nothing goes wrong, can be manumitted in an orderly manner, but which fate or luck or chance, can foreclose on you without warning. (P. 140)

All was going reasonably well with this marriage, on the superficial level of relationships that Temple can create, until one day the past is disinterred. Pete is the kid brother of Red, no doubt physically suggestive of him, probably younger than Red by many years because he is described as looking younger than she remembered Red as being eight years earlier. He comes with some letters that he has found, her passionate letters to the man whose body she had loved. They are not the sort of letters that a woman would want her husband to know she had ever written to a man, Temple explains: the implication is clear that they were not letters of love but of sexuality; they must have been erotic, even pornographic. The fact is that between herself and Red only one force drew them together, her burning desire to be possessed by him, his willingness to play the role, do his job, and evidently his abilities to do it very well.

It would have been a simple matter to pay the few dollars, or the few hundred, for the letters, and be done with Pete; give him the money and off with him. More difficult for Temple would have been to confess to the only person who could have cared about the letters, her own husband, but inasmuch as they were not public figures they could hardly have been blackmailed. If this is Temple's original plan, however, it goes wrong when she confronts Pete. He is Red again, a younger and perhaps, from the vantage point of her own age, an even more attractive version. In reminding her of Red, Pete reawakens her sensuality and makes her realize that she has never had the frenzied joy of sexuality since Red. It is once again the irony of the social class system that marked Lord and Lady Chatterley and brought her gratification with the gardener (even his work was earthy, which for the upper class meant dirty, exactly as they saw sex); now the impotence is not in Popeye, but in the proper and respectable white upper-class male of the South, for whom white womanhood is purity and hence asexuality.

The white woman, a sexual being denied her right to that status by the males who turn their lust only to women they despise (black women on the one hand, prostitutes on the other), finds in this uncouth lower-class white youth, petty blackmailer, hanger-on in life, smalltime criminal, all the masculinity that she craves in a man whom she wants to possess her. Pete is more than the reincarnation of Red; he is the lustiness of the letters that speak out as she cannot speak to her husband, and as the gardener was able to speak to Constance Chatterley. But he is also Red reborn and renewed, the man she had wanted to run off with, for whom her lust had brought death, now come back in the form of a younger brother. He had not expected to be offered Temple but only some dollars, almost any amount would have sufficed, in return for the letters. Instead, she offers herself. It is not enough that she wants to have sex with him; she is ready, in fact she implores, prepares, to go off, leaving family, tearing up the entire past, so that she can give her life to the youth. It is a romantic vision, for she does not foresee how he will quickly tire of her as soon as the money runs out and want to go on to another woman, and another, and another. He is flattered and fascinated by the momentary thrust that she is making, by the sacrifice that she appears to adumbrate, by the desires that she demonstrates when she begs to be possessed. Unlike Ethan Frome, there is no love here, and no rationality either; she is driven by her passions into actions in which her future is deliberately unexamined.

And the death, and Nancy? Nancy alone rises to the occasion. The husband knows nothing of what is taking place; in a sense, he is not on the scene, effaced, ignorant, as impotent a factor in her relationships with the family as Popeye had been in the physical and sexual sense of that word. Only Nancy can see that Temple is driving herself as well as her husband and children to destruction; she knows how shallow is the passion that binds the woman to the youth, how quickly it will dissipate. She sees the two children as victims. Nancy implores Temple to relinquish the man and her plan to run off with him. They confront each other, and she is Temple's double and yet her opposite. Both have had experiences in their sexual pasts which have bound them together, which have in fact been responsible for Nancy's becoming the woman whom Temple could bring into her house to take care of her son, and then both children. Temple could look at Nancy and see herself, all that was degrading about her memories, and find companionship and solace in one who shared in the struggle to be uplifted. But they are different: Temple is rich and upper-class and white, Nancy is poor and lower-class and black. Temple is pulled by the magnetic forces of evil, or those she defines as evil, that reside within her, Nancy only by beneficence. Temple appears as the embodiment of goodness to the world, while within she is its opposite; Nancy is the black dope fiend, whore, and alcoholic who is all goodness, even to the point of being saintly.

Nancy's entreaties fail. She hides the money so that Temple cannot run off with the youth, but that does not stay Temple's determination to abandon her family and have Pete. Nancy offers money to Pete if he will only go off by himself, but again in vain. They are ready to make their getaway in the night. Desperate, Nancy goes into the baby's room and suffocates the infant, apparently by holding a pillow over her head until the last breath of life is gone, and then returns to tell Temple that her child is dead. The family has been saved, but it is a smaller unit: there are now three where before there were five.

All of this Temple narrates, haltingly, seeking at times to avoid some of the more sordid details of both the immediate past and the past past. Temple knows that, in a broader view of moral responsibility, Nancy is not guilty of killing the child. There were more than mitigating circumstances. If there is a murderer to be named, it must be Temple herself. Conscience-stricken, not for the dead child but for the woman about to be sacrificed, Temple pleads with the governor. The governor listens, sometimes incredulous, never doubting the truth of the story, but his is a political decision, and a racial one, too. There is no way that he can afford to tell the world that he is pardoning or even saving the life of a black woman who killed a white baby. What would he be able to say? And at what political cost to his career? Here Faulkner displays his contempt for the morality of the old South, even the emerging new South, but it is hardly likely that the governor's decision would have been any different elsewhere in America, or even the world.

Temple Drake's mission fails, and in that sense hers is a lost search for redemption. That she suffers in making her confession, after having been protected by the veil of secrecy that Nancy had thrown over the entire affair, cannot be denied. But consider how she does it, not merely as a last-minute and too-late pang of conscience after remaining silent throughout the trial, not only requiring proddings to reveal what she is seeking to keep from divulging, but in a private setting where no one will know the depth of her sins. She is no Hester Prynne, wearing the scarlet A for all to point at and scorn. Even her husband has not been made privy to her machinations, lusts, and desires, except by the fact of his being an eavesdropper, carefully concealed behind a curtain. She can save Nancy by confessing to the world, but to the end she has no urge to sacrifice herself to gain redemption. She cannot leave the governor's mansion with a smile on her face and, like Lord Jim, go unflinchingly to her demise, because she has only implicated herself in such a manner that that demise can be avoided. In the end she is still saving her own hide, and that she is pretending to do otherwise only makes the redemption less convincing and the expiation more hypocritical.

Furthermore, and in this Faulkner may have hidden a lesson on expiation that is more profound because it is so obscure, Temple's confession is a sham, because she fails to recognize priorities of responsibilities and consequences. She is more guilt-ridden over her passions than over acts that are replete with evil. The pornographic letters, the fact that she enjoyed sex with Red and wanted it with Pete, these are the matters that trouble her. She is like a schoolboy who is contrite because he has stolen a baseball glove and ball, and who casually mentions in passing that in so doing he has also killed the storekeeper. All that she is able to regret about her past is her sexuality; she is ashamed of having become a sexual woman. As a minor matter she happens to mention with no great difficulty, with no sign of regret, the one great act of evil that she had committed: her perjured testimony on the witness stand when she pointed to an innocent man and sent him to his death. She does not tell this to her uncle or to the governor as the overwhelming sin that she must expiate; it is glossed over as not immediately germane to the problem of the pardon.

How can one expiate one's sins if the greatest of them are thought of as small, and the small ones as great? There is no redemption here because she has failed, not in her mission—that, too, but it is supererogatory—but because she has not recognized, confessed, and dared to examine the nature of the most evil act of her past and the most evil part of her soul. Nancy will go to her death for the murder of the child, and in a literal sense she is the one who committed the act, but Temple will go on in life, a woman who cannot rise because she does not know the nature of her fall. Who is going to pay for the murder of Lee, when the guilty person is only concerned about her salacious letters and her sexual improprieties?

If Faulkner has a message on redemption, and it appears that he has, this is it. One is not redeemed for minor acts, by slight catharsis, for a little cleansing of a small part of one's being, while the greater, the greatest evil lies untouched, unrevealed, unseen, unrecognized. There is not even the ambivalence here that Lord Jim felt about the abandonment of the men, women, and children of the *Patna,* nor the remorse for the error that he had made, the miscalculation, which had resulted in the death of Dain Waris. It is only when people recognize and admit the enormity of their evil deeds that expiation is possible. All other recognition serves merely as diversion, dissembling, concealment for the greater sins beneath. Faulkner's Temple is never redeemed, because she has never learned for what acts she is seeking redemption. Nor will humanity be redeemed, unless there is similar recognition followed by complete expiation.

Nonetheless, this somber interpretation of Temple Drake is not widely shared. Literary critic Leslie Fiedler does find Temple redeemed. The redemption takes place through the self-sacrifice of Nancy, so that Temple is "left at the play's end aching with a higher lust for religious belief, about to follow her husband home."[2] And Frohock finds her expiation "morally appropriate," but he does not question whether the expiation is actually effected.[3]

Another critic, Joseph Gold, reminds us that Nancy, like Christ, is executed on Friday, but we need little reminder that she is a deliberately created Christ in fiction. By her act of murder, Gold contends, Nancy "enables Temple to change the course of her life and come to grips with reality and to terms with herself before God."[4] One wonders if Christ enabled humanity to change its course—enabled, perhaps, but this does not mean that humanity succeeded in doing what had been made possible for it to do.

There is, however, redemption in the story, and the key to it is in the title of the second novel. The nun for whom a requiem is to be held, or for whom the entire work is a requiem, is of course Nancy. She embodies all that is despised, or at least was at the time, in a small town in Mississippi, but Faulkner canonizes her. She is not a saint like Hugo's Jean Valjean, because she is believable in her saintliness, even godliness, of virtue. It is not merely that she has fallen and risen again. The message of Faulkner in the portrait of Nancy is more profound. She had never fallen. That she was a whore, dope fiend, and alcoholic, and deserving of the other epithets, labels, and pejoratives heaped upon her, is irrelevant to the matter of goodness or evil, so it cannot be said that she has risen from levels that were low. Hers is not salvation through pollution, because the alleged pollution is only that, it is a sham evil viewed from the moral stance of amoral people. Nancy does not rise from the gutters, because she has never been in them, except in the most literal and narrow sense.

In that she is willing to die for the sins of another, she is a Christlike figure, but even more Christlike than Christ for she is not so much claiming goodness as she is concealing that she is martyr and self-sacrificing. Her sacrifice is only possible if she goes to her death with her secret intact. She is so holy that she does not even conceive of herself as holy. She sings in joy to the heavens, because she has saved a small portion of humanity; she is not joyous because of her pride in accomplishment, but in the goal that was reached. This is humanity redeemed.

Nancy is to be killed for Temple's sins. She is confident that she will rise again, but it will be in Heaven, not on earth. Like the execution of Christ, hers will take place on a Friday in springtime, but to this inescapable analogy Faulkner has let it be known that she is scheduled to die on March 13th. Good Friday thus becomes Friday the thirteenth: the religion of the Western world is reenacted in an aura of ignorance, violence, stupidity, hatred, and superstition.

As she goes to her death, Nancy offers solace to Temple, a lost person who asks, "What about me?" Supposing there is nobody waiting in the tomorrows to forgive, then what, Nancy, Temple implores. Believe, Nancy replies, as she moves on after the jailor, toward the executioner:

> TEMPLE: Believe what, Nancy? Tell me.
> NANCY: Believe.

NOTES

1. W. M. Frohock, *The Novel of Violence in America,* 2nd ed. (Dallas: Southern Methodist University Press, 1957), p. 164.

2. Leslie Fiedler, *Love and Death in the American Novel* (New York: Criterion Books, 1960), p. 314.

3. Frohock, *Novel of Violence,* p. 159.

4. Joseph Gold, *William Faulkner: A Study in Humanism from Metaphor to Discourse* (Norman: University of Oklahoma Press, 1966), p. 98.

8

Six Literary Images for Criminologists to Ponder

The six characters who have been discussed hardly present a unified vision of transgression and suffering, expiation, absolution, and atonement, either imposed from without or developing from within. They are not meant to be a single image, and they do not fail us because of occasional, even frequent, and sometimes sharp divergence. Philosophic, literary, and humanistic approaches to life and society are the creations of single individuals, not of what can be called a discipline. Yet, to see these only as six visions, discrete, unrelated, falling short at any point of integration into a single message, would be to underplay their significance. It would ignore the continuity in humanistic thought which is surely as prominent as in scientific thought, although the social sciences are not as cumulatively continuous as are the natural or hard sciences.

The six authors come from different periods and societies. The Russian and the Frenchman were contemporaries. Two were British, yet not exactly, for Conrad was a Pole by birth and early education, and although he wrote in English, Polish was his mother tongue. Further, Conrad and Defoe were separated by almost two centuries. Finally, two were American, at least a generation apart and in other ways dissimilar: Wharton was female, Yankee, and upper-class; Faulkner was male, a Southerner at a time when regionalism was strong as a factor distinguishing some Americans from others, and not from a moneyed aristocracy. So that, although Sophocles, Kafka, or Camus might have given us a wider range, the spectrum is not narrow in the six authors here discussed.

What unites several of them is their rejection of the criminal as inherently evil. Only Moll Flanders is a completely unacceptable person, offering an image of a human being devoid of moral integrity, compassion, ability to understand the enormity of crime, and willingness to reform through suffering. All others suffer, albeit in different ways, for different reasons, and with different meanings.

True, Moll has not committed any acts as frightful as the murders of Raskolnikov, nor has she inflicted as great suffering upon others as Ethan Frome or Temple Drake. She is more pickpocket, sneak thief, petty and not so petty larcenist, shoplifter, confidence artist, and swindler than she is violent, assaultive, or homicidal. All this may be slightly mitigating, in the sense that Defoe is offering a limited view of the criminal, or of a subcategory of criminal. If she does not atone but lives on the fruits of her labor and the rewards for her delicts, she is almost but not quite rogue rather than criminal. Rogue, perhaps, but never a likable one; it is hardly possible for a reader to chuckle with her, as one does with Tom Jones, Felix Krull, or Lafcadio. In that her crimes are numerous, that she is a career criminal, she represents an important, probably increasing, and socially threatening portion of humanity. To the extent that these crimes are individually and even cumulatively lacking in the enormity of the acts committed by Dostoevsky's and Faulkner's characters, Moll Flanders would not present a central concern of modern criminology. But probably without the slightest prescience of portraying a world about to be born, Defoe may have painted in Moll a portrait of the modern criminal: she is completely amoral, devoid of any loyalties at all, lacking the intellectual depths to work out justifications for her rejections of the norms of society, able to blame others for her fate while enjoying it at the same time, and interested only in the successful development of her criminal career. Her concern is not to be caught, not to be punished.

Moll may reflect early effects of modernity in the European world. As Defoe depicts her, she is not enmeshed in the solidarities and dynamics of a collective communal life typical of family, village, or neighborhood. Her moral truancy is both the result and the source of her alienation, and she uses it for her own liberation. But her alienation is not bitter or deeply felt; it is alienation with a smile, a smugness lacking the moral reflexes and discontent we have come to associate with the politically and socially sophisticated.

Moll might stand as a harbinger of the modern social actor to come, an individual caught up in a confusing social skein of too many choices and too many opportunities. She migrates through a succession of widely divergent worlds during her odyssey, none of which becomes home. Defoe's book is a devastating examination of upheaval and its repercussions on the individual: there is mobility and rootlessness which bring with them amorality. The anomic threat of life lived in highly discrepant and often conflicting milieux is portrayed by Defoe as a kind of uprootedness in which the individual constantly alternates values and attitudes because the only concrete reality in a world of flux and changing constellations of values is the self. The private sphere takes precedence over the public and provides a shelter from the threats of anonymity.

Moll as the self-seeking and self-aggrandizing egoist contrasts sharply and pathetically with the tragic and heroic images of Lord Jim and Raskolnikov. Her worst sin is moral crudity; were she disdainful and filled with scorn, she could at least engender some respectful feelings for her rebelliousness and refusal to accept a world of piety and injustice. Rather, she makes her accommodations, and her spirit congeals before us.

Unlike Moll, Jim and Raskolnikov are filled with doubt, uncertainty, and often despair. They are never sure of motives, and life is tragic for them to the degree that it is filled with prodigious complications. Consciousness overwhelms conscience. Perhaps that is the message and warning of Defoe: as the social world becomes increasingly complex, capable of tolerating many points of view, the psychic structure of the individual disintegrates. Raskolnikov and Jim are caught up in a swirl of possibilities—their minds breed inexhaustible and incalculable feelings and ideas; they are victimized, even paralyzed, by the plurality of social worlds and the variety of roles to inhabit and of beliefs to embrace.

In contrast to Moll, Raskolnikov and Jim are thoughtful, animated by a sense of responsibility; unlike them, she is never passive or disarmed before the massive, complex, accumulated ethical substance of the world. Moll is the "other-directed" personality par excellence, and it is the contemplative types such as Raskolnikov and Jim who are displaced in the modern world. They represent archaic personality types.

Nevertheless, Defoe could not completely denude his protagonist of eighteenth-century liberal vanities: she is the protomodern, and her freedom is in her defiance, not in her participation. All she lacks to make her utterly modern, or at least bring her up to the nineteenth-century conception of modernity, is a sense of guilt. With guilt, conscience appears. In the secular world of the twentieth century, Moll would not be lost, as were Mr. K. and Meursault, and as for Raskolnikov and Jim, they would be doomed.

In Raskolnikov and Jim we witness the promotion of guilt, its degrees, nuances, imputations, tact, and finally its full expression in self-righteousness in which there are accusations without accusers, tribunals without judges, and verdicts without juries. To be oneself both accuser and accused is to be alienated, but it may be the birth of conscience. Moll feels no sense of self-condemnation.

Hence, for Moll there was no need to suffer. She contrasts with Raskolnikov, who is warned by Sonya that he must suffer in order to live again, but Moll must avoid suffering in order to continue to live, whether it is during her years of criminality or upon retirement. Conscience is nowhere present in Moll; there is not even a glimpse that she is aware that such a force exists, except for a fleeting feeling which she quickly overcomes. There is no catharsis, because she experiences no need for it. She goes into retirement to live well (no doubt a stalwart member of the community, a contributor to charitable causes, a staunch opponent of bleeding heart liberal softness toward criminals) off the proceeds that she has accumulated through a lifetime of criminality and fraud. If she writes her memoirs, instead of having them written for her by Defoe, it is to accumulate more money by capitalizing on the crimes that she has committed (perhaps she will earn a little on the side, by usury). Well, Defoe wrote the tale, not Moll, or at least so the reader is led to believe—that it is a novel presented in the first person as if it were the old woman's own story—but one can be certain that she received a good percentage of the royalties: she was not one to be outwitted when it came to making a good bargain.

In fact, the memoirs of Moll remind one of the stream of funds, in advances, royalties, and lecture fees from universities, being paid to white-collar and other upper-class criminals. Publishers and broadcasters take their own moralistic stance, avoiding responsibility as conspirators, by disarmingly and unconvincingly declaring that they do no more than give the public what it wants (but they create the wants of the public, feed on these wants and feed them, continuing so long as the profits flow, all without regard to morality or consequences). Moll Flanders is getting her rewards, as other criminals have obtained theirs as well.

The penitence of Moll Flanders is blatantly false. Whether Defoe saw it in that form and was being ironic can be debated, but it is strikingly similar to the penitence of persons in high places, counting their money by the hundreds of thousands, perhaps millions, of dollars, money that came to them both from their transgressions and the public exploitation of their notoriety. By money and perhaps by some nicely placed charities, they will regain standing, and if the contributions are large enough, university halls will be named for them, and hospitals, too.

Moll Flanders begs comparison with Ethan Frome. Moll is not searching for absolution, because she is unable to recognize wrongdoing; Ethan is not making the search, because after recognizing his wrong he resigned himself to a fate where absolution is beyond his reach. Defoe has offered a pessimistic view of humanity, because his transgressor is without conscience and morality. She lives to enjoy the luxuries of old age (enjoy, not suffer in penitence) with her accumulated loot. She has renounced criminality, not because it is evil but because it was no longer necessary for her to feed her coffers. She does not have to suffer to live again, she has to avoid suffering.

Wharton's image is equally pessimistic, because for much less evil intent Ethan Frome is doomed to a life in which there can be no end to the suffering. Complete expiation is beyond attainment. Even the message with which Dostoevsky concludes *Crime and Punishment,* the glimpse of a new life that will be reached by Raskolnikov, is absent from Wharton. Both Defoe and Wharton, each unlike the other, give us a world of gloom: one because the transgressors are triumphant, laughing in mockery at all of us, and the other because they are doomed and no amount of suffering will be sufficient for them to earn their redemption. In either instance, the world is bereft of hope.

Moll Flanders comes off scot-free, and at first glance she may in that respect be an early portrait of a Temple Drake. Not exactly, although there are strands that unite them. Whatever remorse Temple feels, she is not made to suffer except inwardly, as does Lord Jim with his self-imposed burden. Like Jim, she tries to run away, but the pending execution for which she shares responsibility follows her. Like the memory of the *Patna,* it cannot be effaced by flight. But Temple is never punished by society, for she allows another, in fact others, to accept that fate, and like Moll she will live again without absolution, something that distinguishes both from Raskolnikov.

Yet Temple differs from the others, and in this sense she has much in common with modern criminals in that she is both victim and victimizer. Of course, all offenders can be said to be victims, and seldom has this been more forcefully demonstrated than in Raskolnikov. But not only in him, for all of the characters in this volume are victims as much as Temple, insofar as the offender has been brought to his position of committing the wrongful deeds by unfortunate social, environmental, even biological circumstances, said by many to be beyond control. This ultradeterminist view is neither improper nor irrelevant, for to the extent that it can be shown that these were indeed important factors in bringing the individual to the point where he commits his crime, it may permit sufficient restructuring of society, families, education, and general environment to prevent others from reaching the same position and performing similar acts. It is a utopian dream, no doubt, but not without some possibilities of being partially effected—enough perhaps to save some persons from becoming offenders and others from becoming the objects of their offenses. Our numerous social programs, to a limited extent at least, are directed toward crime prevention by just such palliative measures. In this respect, Temple is somewhat less a victim than others, but in another sense she is much more so. Except for the brutalities that occurred at the moonshiners' place and the tragicomic absurdities to which she was subjected in the Memphis brothel, she cannot find exculpation of her behavior in social conditions or in the activities of others. Only someone completely denying any free will could come to a conclusion that she is absolved, and then everyone would have to be absolved for everything.

Moll Flanders, too, can be shown as victim, but to reach such a conclusion one resorts to the determinist view of the world. She was a product of the life forces that molded her from the moment that she was born in Newgate, hardly an auspicious beginning, although even this is utilized by her to gain an inheritance from the woman whom she discovers to be her mother. Ethan Frome, who evokes sympathy in us, is likewise the tragic result of a desolate life, a dreary existence with a complaining and bitter woman whom he has taken as wife, and he will pay because he sought to abandon her by his suicide ride.

Temple might be accused of being a not entirely unwilling victim, and indeed few characters in fiction have been subjected to the anguish that she suffers in the rape by the impotent Popeye. Some crimes, particularly homicides but not entirely excluding rape, have been described as victim-precipitated, in that the victim has deliberately played a role in an interactional relationship that culminated in the crime.[1] Close examination, however, fails to reveal that this is relevant to Temple. She did not precipitate the rape—in fact, many criminologists as well as feminists reject the entire notion that victim precipitation can be applied to the crime of rape. Nor did she precipitate the fateful meeting with Red's brother Pete, although here she is more seducer than seduced. Is she, then, not the victim of the murder of her infant? In every homicide, the family is victim as much as the person who has been murdered, or at least in those in which the murderer is not the spouse or some other family member.

In the instance of Temple, however, she is not victimized by the death of the child, for this is precisely what saves her. She is the beneficiary of the slaying. It is designed to hold intact her marriage, her family, her relationship with the older child: in short to make it possible for her life to continue. A sacrifice has been made, or a double sacrifice, the life of the little girl and of her killer, but Temple did not plan or choose the road of sacrifice. She was merely the recipient of the good emanating from it, the sole such recipient.

On a tangent, it is an irony here that Faulkner comes into such sharp conflict with Dostoevsky. For Raskolnikov learns that murder is never justified, it is its own evil and begets other evil, no matter what rationalizations in the mind of the murderer bring him to commit the act; Faulkner arranges his choreography in such a manner that the justification of the murder is never combatted, never denied, and that the murder begets good, not further evil.

For all that, Temple is a victim. She is both victim and victimizer, in two entirely different sets of acts, related as they are to each other. She never lashes out at the persons responsible for her fate; on the contrary, she protects one and marries the other. However, she does create victims, as much as any offender who walks around with a loaded gun and murders an innocent storekeeper or customer during a holdup. In the abduction following the rape, she arranges, unwittingly and unwillingly (both important as mitigation), the sequence of events that culminate in the murder of Red. In the courtroom, with deliberation, she sends an innocent man to his death. And eight years later, she pursues a course of sexual self-indulgence that brings Nancy to the point of infanticide.

Temple does not begin to understand the nature of her wrongdoing and uses a cathartic cop-out so that she can return to a full life, if not on the day of the crucifixion, then not too long after. She will not be one of the apostles witnessing the resurrection, nor will she be setting aside even twenty-four hours of denial for atonement.

This is not to deny that, in the total setting that Faulkner creates, Temple will regret, even suffer a bit, because of Nancy's fate. But it will be Nancy's fate, not Temple's, and it is hardly consistent with the latter's character that the suffering will be endless, like that of Ethan Frome. She will shed tears over Nancy and will know the part she has played in her execution, but she can never recognize the evil that she has wrought in life and may continue to bring forth, and she cannot undergo suffering as a means for the regeneration of life. She is not a Raskolnikov, for whom the punishment was in the crime, who had killed himself in killing the pawnbroker, and she does not have the sense of lost honor of Jim, unable to come to full life until the opportunity for complete redemption has arisen.

Temple Drake stands somewhat aside from, rather than on a continuum between, Ethan Frome and Moll Flanders, or Ethan Frome and Lord Jim. She will not revel in the rewards of her crimes, as does Moll; they will not make her later years happier ones. But she will not be reborn as a whole person, because although she has fallen, as did Raskolnikov, she does not know the nature of that fall. She too has died, for every murderer kills himself, but she is unaware of her own death. Unlike Ethan, she will not live in a circle of hopeless doom, because Ethan Frome had no Christ to die for him. Nancy dies for Temple's sins, and if Temple only knew what those sins were, her Christ might not have died in vain. Here Faulkner may be raising a question terrible to contemplate: humanity knows that Christ died, but do we know why, or for what evil deeds? Are the sins only cleansed, not effaced; are they nothing more than treated cathartically, so that, with a new slate, mankind can start to sin again and hope that there will be new Christs, a second coming, and a third, and countless more?

Faulkner, then, joins with Defoe and Wharton, although in a most dissimilar way, in giving us a pessimistic view of the human condition, and in so doing Temple is a more devastating image of humanity than either Moll Flanders or Ethan Frome. In this mosaic, Jean Valjean offers little to the social scientist seeking to understand and to cope with crime and violence, immorality and inhumanity, as they are manifested in a world a century after Hugo wrote. Valjean does suffer, but unjustly; he is redeemed, but was never in need of it. His is not an image of the criminal, but of the injustice of a society that hounds a good man. Like Lord Jim, he must have gone to his death smiling and unflinching, but there the similarity ends, for Jim's final moments are very different from those of Valjean. Jim knows that he committed a dishonorable act in his youth, and redemption comes when he is willing and able to face those who have lost faith in him, an ability that arises from acceptance of responsibility.

Like Lord Jim, Jean Valjean is haunted and hunted, but more from without than from within. When Jim is told that no one cares any longer about what happened on the *Patna,* he cannot accept this because he himself cares. But Valjean has the reverse problem; the outside world has lost faith in him, and finally, when he confesses that he is an escaped convict, the loss of faith even extends to his adoptive daughter and her husband. On his deathbed he is forgiven and finally accepted (absolution on the deathbed is of course a common enough experience, symbolized by the last rites) but not because he is dying. The acceptance comes from those who have the strongest affectional ties and with whom he has interwoven his life. That Marius offers this forgiveness for the wrong reason seems to concern neither Valjean nor Hugo, although it should be important to the reader.

For Hugo, it is the fact of love and acceptance that is significant, and having received it one can die. But if it does not matter whether it arises from base, false, or selfish motives, then it will have little relevance for the vision of transgression and rebirth. What moral regeneration can be anticipated if people hold out their hands to the transgressor (in this instance falsely accused, persecuted, pilloried, a man heroic and saintly) not because they recognize the wholeness of the person, his basic humanity and the frailty that as a human being he possesses, but for reasons so artificial and irrelevant that, by implication, humanity is being denied? Cosette and Marius do not forgive because Jean Valjean has repented and repaid, suffered and atoned, changed and been reborn, and hence can walk again among all men and women, nor do they accept because they recognize that the imputed transgressor has committed no wrongs, that he is a good person as he was in the past, and that he should never have been an outcast. Forgiveness comes to Jean Valjean from his daughter and son-in-law because on a previous occasion he has been the young man's benefactor, and when this incident from their biographies is discovered, he can be embraced. It is almost like the organized crime figure who should be seen in terms of goodness because he is a nice father and a decent grandfather. The recognition that Marius has, and the reason he rushes to Jean Valjean, might be likened to a move by a religious organization that, having received a substantial contribution from Moll Flanders, makes her a respected and honored member of the parish or congregation, perhaps even naming a bench for her in perpetuity—alas, a not infrequent occurrence, in these days of fiscal crises when money is so hard to come by legally and ethically, and contributions, like gift horses, are unlikely to be examined for dental or other defects.

In sum, then, modern criminality has given humanity many persons of the type of Moll Flanders, and occasionally a Temple Drake. Examples of those who have suffered like Ethan Frome are not at all unknown. Few criminals are to be found who cannot live without redemption or who cannot be reborn without suffering: men and women like Lord Jim and Raskolnikov are as rare as saints like Jean Valjean and Christs like Nancy. Is Raskolnikov, then, so uncommon as to be atypical? Must one conclude that little is to be learned from him, however profoundly analyzed and presented, about the minds of most criminals, even if a great deal is learned about the minds of a small number?

Actually, Raskolnikov is not in all respects so dissimilar from these others, and in certain ways he is most relevant to an understanding of the mind of the transgressor. In this entire genre of literature, from the great Greek tragedies to the Elizabethan drama and the beginnings of the novel, the characters seek to escape from responsibility by placing blame for their conduct on some force outside themselves. Outside can here include inside, for it can be the devil within, an inner compulsion that one cannot control, but it is outside the "true self" in the sense that the decision to do or to refrain from doing is one that the individual defines himself as incapable of making or of having made. As Raskolnikov and others demonstrate, suffering and atonement, and consequently rebirth, are possible only if one rejects such a cop-out.

The Russian critic and philosopher Vyacheslav Ivanov goes even further, contending that when Oedipus inflicts punishment upon himself (it is voluntary, almost like Raskolnikov surrendering at a police station when he was in no danger of being apprehended), what Sophocles is arguing is that man must accept responsibility, and hence suffering, for acts that are wrong even though they were destined and inescapable—destiny, in this instance, being symbolized by the fact that they were foretold by the oracle.[2] Moll seeks to excuse herself by taking note of the devil within. His more complex rationalizations aside for the moment, Raskolnikov is overwhelmed as he walks away from the overheard conversation between the soldier and the student by a sense of destiny and doom, a belief that he can no longer control his own actions: all is foreordained. Lord Jim, of course, hesitates, and Conrad has arranged the entire scene on the *Patna* as one in which Jim "finds himself" in the lifeboat, rather than one in which he jumps.[3] Temple Drake does have a sense of guilt, but only for her sexual passions, the "sin" of not being the frigid woman that the Southern whites at the time expected of their proper families. Even Ethan Frome, although he does not run away from the fate that befalls him after Mattie has been crippled, is never able to articulate that he is himself the architect of his later life and of the wrongs that he has wrought upon himself and others. He recalls that he remembered Zenobia at home, and that is when the sled swerved from its path and resulted in the failure of the double suicide, as if it were this glimmer of kindness and compassion that came from within himself that caused the tragic suffering of the years that followed.

The human being, in the eyes of these writers and many other artists and philosophers, has an infinite capacity for reasoning that he is himself not to blame for the wrongs that he has committed. *The thing happened,* rather than *I did it.* But Raskolnikov must abandon this outlook, if he is to suffer and through suffering to live again. Jim must likewise know that he jumped, not that he found himself in the lifeboat, and must know not only that he performed the act, which was morally reprehensible, but that it was within his power to avoid it.

There is, then, an existential message on crime running through these works, and it is found in Balzac, Stendhal, Flaubert, and down to our moderns, Richard Wright, James Baldwin, Albert Camus, and of course more than in any other, Jean-Paul Sartre. Its theme is most carefully articulated in Dostoevsky, but is seen in almost as sharp relief in Conrad as well: no act is a free one, of a free individual, if that person places blame for it on fate, destiny, determinism, inner compulsions, other people, society, or environment, and if that individual cannot accept that he committed the act as a voluntary one. Then, if the behavior is legally outlawed, morally wrong, and indefensible, one must not only be able to accept the guilt for its commission but also be willing to recognize its evil and suffer as a consequence of having perpetrated it, in order to be redeemed.

Redemption requires suffering, not in order to rehabilitate or to deter, as criminologists have argued for years (and it would seem that it seldom rehabilitates and only weakly deters), but because, as Sonya understands, those who have fallen cannot hope to rise and live again unless they have suffered. The soul must be cleansed, the individual chastised, the evil expiated. This is the tale of Lazarus: he did rise from the dead. When Raskolnikov states that it was not the pawnbroker and her sister whom he had killed but himself, he was insisting that the suffering by the criminal is in the crime itself, not in the treatment by society; and he is further stating that one cannot rise from the dead unless one has died, and that he had. In the language of St. Paul, the final experience of sin is recounted in the past: "Once you were dead in your sins, but now . . ." Death, which is the ordinary experience of human beings, is preeminently the future event. Here death is in the past.

For Raskolnikov, and hence for Dostoevsky, there is no self-expiation or self-atonement. To be just is to be declared just, to be counted as just: it is the verdict of ultimate acquittal. The supreme sin is to justify oneself, and it is one that fell heavily upon Raskolnikov.

The suffering that Raskolnikov underwent in Siberia was at the hands of society, both organized society and its outlaws, his fellow-prisoners; but the agony had started the moment the crime was committed, and even before, when with heavy heart he walked away from the soldier and the student convinced that he was fated to carry out his murderous plan. Yet all the agony, before his arrest and after, that seethed within him could not have cleansed his soul, made him a new person, given him a rebirth, unless there were hardships, deprivations and imprisonment, in addition to conscience together with realization and admission of wrongdoing.

Motivations for criminal behavior are complex, and nowhere are they encountered in greater complexities than in the mind of Raskolnikov. They exist on conscious and unconscious levels, and sometimes they are rationalized in such a manner that the perpetrator himself does not know the reason that brought about his actions. Raskolnikov had a superman theory of humanity, felt that he was one of the chosen who could decide who must live and whose life was dispensable so that death would only be a benefit to the surviving human beings. Here one has motive, but on examination it appears that there are two motives. On the one hand, he wanted to eliminate "a louse," so that humanity would benefit by her death; yet, even stronger in his motivation, he wanted to carry out a murder so that he would prove to himself that he was one of the chosen. By slaying Alëna he would establish to himself that he was not an ordinary man. Were these intertwined goals only rationalizations, to conceal from himself the true avarice behind the act? He was living in penury, starving, unable to face his landlady, as the reader is informed in the opening passages of the book. He did want to benefit monetarily from the crime. He would steal the goods that Alëna had—usuriously, it is emphasized—accumulated. Thus are criminal motives recondite, arcane, consisting of intricate layers one uses to conceal from the perpetrator another motive, little understood by the offender, no less by the world around him.

Motives are reasons that set people on a path to goals. What happened to the goals that Raskolnikov sought? In eliminating the pawnbroker he found that he "had to" kill her sister Lizaveta as well because the sister chanced to come home before he departed, although he had carefully planned to carry out the murder at a time when Lizaveta would not be there. So the original goal was perverted: there were two murders where one had been planned. He now had sufficient funds to take care of his needs but he was unable to benefit from his crime, hiding the jewels, giving some money away. More important, from the time that he killed he lost faith in himself as a human being, found that he was not one of the select but one of the fallen and that in carrying out the murder he had proven not that he was chosen to decide the fate of others but that he was unworthy of deciding the fate of himself.

A crime cannot be confined. That is the meaning of the death of Lizaveta, and it is a message that has far-reaching importance for criminology. Raskolnikov plans a crime which he is convinced will benefit humanity, and the logic of his action leads him to commit another, the evil of which even he cannot defend. In Dostoevsky's image, this is because the original act is evil in itself, independent of its consequences or its loftiest motivations. That is why one cannot control the pathways that crime will take, once it has been condoned; nor can one control the victims that crime will bring in its wake, the good who will be eliminated with the putatively bad.

Raskolnikov walks into the police station and gives himself up for two reasons: he has suffered unbearably since he committed the crime, and in that sense the surrender is to reduce the anguish; and, by contrast, he has escaped the official deprivations that society demands and imposes, and Sonya has convinced him that there is no other road if he is to walk again among human beings and be reborn. Yet can we recognize the criminal, the modern murderer, in Raskolnikov, or is this an idealized and romanticized vision with little relevance to a sordid reality?

Let us link Raskolnikov in his surrender and his acceptance of the verdict that he must suffer with a few others. There is Lord Jim: his escape is not like that of the other officers of the *Patna,* for conscience hangs heavy on him, and he is forever burdened by the memory of his dishonorable deed. Follow this with Ethan Frome, accepting his destiny with hopeless resignation. Finally Nancy, but not Temple: Nancy going joyously to her death, believing that she has saved some others who, because of her, will be able to live.

Where are these types of criminals among the transgressors in the modern world? Whom do they represent? What universality is there in such persons? Are they not a quartet so glorified that, even before we add Jean Valjean to the list, they are more noble in their ethics, more decent in their adherence to principles, than the mass of humanity, of people who never murder or abandon a ship with its hundreds of persons who will almost certainly meet their death? Are they not a niche above most mortals, and far above the offenders who are the objects of criminological studies?

The fact is that murderers are not walking into police stations to surrender when they are not suspects and when they know that there is insufficient evidence to convict them. They are not propelled to such self-sacrifice by their inability to live without paying for their misdeed. On the contrary, they are well able to live, and their major concern appears to be the search for methods to escape apprehension, or if apprehended, to construct mechanisms for buying or lying their way out of their fix, and if that cannot be done, to make a bargain with prosecutors and with society. There are many killers but few Raskolnikovs among us, it can be argued.

Moll Flanders, in all her banality, may be the most accurate or at least the most representative of our common criminals, and Temple Drake may have more typicality than the unusual circumstances and contrived plot would suggest. It is Moll's lack of nobility that comes through, and in Temple one confronts the criminal who is weak-willed and will satisfy what little conscience is present by a small effort in the direction of catharsis, or by a carefully controlled, self-inflicted humiliation, the limits of which are tightly drawn. However profoundly Dostoevsky has looked into the mind of the murderer, or Conrad into the world of a man devastated by the loss of his own self-esteem, in the end, it is argued, it will be a false vision of transgression that we receive if we confuse Raskolnikov and Lord Jim with the criminals around us.

The problem may be that Dostoevsky and Conrad, unlike Camus and Faulkner, had visions of humanity unrelated to crime and punishment as it is acted out in the last years of the twentieth century.

What, then, can criminology learn from the literary masters, if the characters they have created and described are so far removed from the realities of everyday criminality? A great deal—and it is possible that our limited progress in understanding crime is due to our limited assimilation of these lessons.

To start, it may be that crime is not always its own punishment, as Dostoevsky contended, but it can be, and only then can punishment be effective. Crime is not its own punishment for Moll Flanders, but it is for Raskolnikov, and if it is not for Meursault in Camus' *The Stranger,* it is for Bigger Thomas in Wright's *Native Son.* These works can be explained not only in terms of the view of humanity held by the authors but also in the characters they created, their socialization, rationalizations, alienation, and sense of or need for community. Individuals with a profound sense of morality, with deep commitments to community and society, with belief in a humanistic and/or religious ideal (the two may even be fused, although there is a strand of humanism that specifically separates them), contend that humanity is its own justification and that, as human beings, we must start from the premise that human life is good, meaningful, and worthwhile. Such persons will find in their criminality the seeds of their own destruction. A man like Lord Jim, in contrast to the others in the lifeboat, will feel alienated from the world and hence destroyed—or his self-image is destroyed—by whatever he may do that he himself defines as evil. Moll Flanders and Meursault had no ties to the community, the former because she was the all-for-oneself criminal, the latter because he was the everlasting stranger or outsider in a world to which he was indifferent and which reciprocated with hostility, as it so often does. Raskolnikov is more complex: he is an alienated person but he has a deep need for society, and though he does not recognize that need within himself it is omnipresent and powerful.

Although the world of criminality has very few Raskolnikovs, Lord Jims, or Nancys, it does have many a Moll Flanders and others as contemptuous of life and as estranged from human society as Meursault. In that view, crime is not its own suffering, but it can be, and literature has indicated the conditions under which it can be, the persons for whom it is, and why it fails to be so for many others.

There is, moreover, a development in these literary works of the theme, itself a humanistic one, that there is nothing inherently ignoble about the criminal but only about those of his acts which are crimes. This is a lesson that runs through all of the great literary images of transgressors, and it is brought into relief by the depiction of these transgressors: Raskolnikov, an essentially noble character, selfless, loving, devoted, and in the end alienated not from his society but from his own evil deed; Jim, a man for whom honor was so vital that he spent his life in search of his own, which he had lost; Ethan Frome, who symbolizes both strength against adversity and the weakness of one unwilling to stand up against what looms as destiny, facing up to the consequences of an act for which he was responsible; Nancy, singing with religious fervor as she faces death and summarizing the idea that, in the soul of one who performs murder and other heinous acts, the noblest of persons can be located. The theme is elucidated in Jean Genet, where the most degrading acts are performed by the purest of persons.

This is an insight that criminologists have not sufficiently pondered: they have confused the person with the act. Semantically, one who commits a murder is a murderer, one who commits a robbery is a robber. There is nothing here but definition, tautology. What the several novelists discussed here have suggested (perhaps all but Defoe) is that one can separate the act from the individual, that the former is a performance, the latter an identity. The good can murder, the honorable can commit the most dishonorable deed. Dostoevsky particularly teaches that the separation of the individual from his conduct is essential if society is to see in each human being an inherent worth, and that each person can be salvaged because he is not evil, although what he has done, on a single occasion or repeatedly, may well be.

The human being has the capacity to fall. It is not a new lesson; it is present in the testaments that have come down with the Judeo-Christian legacy. What the literary masters have depicted is that this capacity is present in all persons, that it is inherent in being human: that it is, in short, the human condition, the human frailty. It is more than hubris, more than the flaw that prevents the human from attaining godlike perfection, it is more than that because it is far worse in its potential. Not all persons will fall; if all did, society would not be possible. But all can, good people and noble ones, and because all can fall, those who follow in the footsteps of Adam or Cain do not cease to be humans with worth even when they commit their basest transgressions.

Man has the capacity to rationalize, to explain away his wrongful deeds, to cathart in order to cover them with a surface-cleansing confession, and particularly to avoid facing the unpleasant reality that the conduct was voluntarily performed by a sane mind having rational motive and control over self. People are blamers, and they can find numerous objects for their blame: society, parents, inner drives beyond control, the victim, or a higher law (the last-named is more justification and rationalization, even reason and rationale, than it is blame). However, no one can hope to make the criminal see that he is essentially, which means in essence, a good person, unless the perpetrator can perceive both that his act was evil and that it was performed voluntarily by a free individual. The acceptance of responsibility, the location of the mechanisms for escape from it, the distinction between cause and reason, cause and motive, cause and justification, have been illuminated by the literary masters as well as by philosophers, and can become central to the contribution that literature makes to criminology. The universality of literary works and their applicability to the modern world teaches us that humanity is capable both of searching for escape from responsibility and of recognizing the errors in that escape; that the path of redemption cannot be walked until such responsibility is assumed can be found in literary works from Sophocles to Sartre.

The most elaborate justification is little more than a mechanism for presenting, not to the world but to oneself, an image of a perpetrator devoid of responsibility. Catharsis is a false cleansing of self; it cannot work. The rationalized motives of Raskolnikov collapse: the more he seeks to retain them, the more confused he becomes about them, the less he believes in them, and most important, the less support he is given by such motives. Instead of proving that he is above ordinary mortals by his ability to carry out the planned and unplanned axings, he proves to himself the very reverse, that he is below them, but because he is below them, he must have fallen below, and therefore he was one of them, and can rise to live with humanity again.

Earlier I took note of a remark by Gilbert Geis, a prominent criminologist, who cited Raskolnikov's as an example of a type of crime that Jeremy Bentham had failed to consider: "a murder [which] is defined, with considerable justification, as a social good by its perpetrator and thus morally justifiable."[4] It is an important point that Geis makes here, and it is particularly relevant to the self-righteous violence so firmly believed in by political terrorists and other politically motivated criminals, including those who are called, at least by their friends and admirers, freedom fighters. If we are for the most part weary of terrorism and frightened by it, how different it often appears in historical perspective. Just look at the terrorist and murderous rebellions of Nat Turner and Denmark Vesey, and perhaps unnamed others who led slave revolts: few would today denounce these people, and few would find their behavior other than justifiable and designed to benefit humanity. In fact, quite the opposite: the American slaves and the Jews under Hitler have often been the subject of criticism, or at least regret, that there was not more resistance on their parts, in the form of political crime, in which murder could not have been excluded, and which would surely have been defined by the perpetrators as a social good.

Yet Raskolnikov does not quite fit as a perfect example of the significant point that Geis is making, for eventually the murderer of Alëna renounces, and with good reason, his former definition of his crime as having been performed to promote some social good. In fact it is only in his renunciation that he can find regeneration possible. But I would turn to Nancy, committing murder for the most altruistic reason and never renouncing her justification nor denouncing her act. She does not merely see the killing as both good and necessary, but is willing to suffer for it. She poses a problem, or Faulkner does, more sharply than Raskolnikov and his creator. What can one say of the person who commits a crime purely for the sake of saving humanity, or a portion thereof—a family group, even a single individual—when the perpetrator believes, with considerable justification, that the outcome will be a social good? What if this is the motive, unsullied by conscious or unconscious excuses and rationalizations used by the individual to conceal the truth from oneself?

Nancy's fate is more of an issue for criminologists than is Raskolnikov's, because neither Nancy nor Faulkner ever renounces the propriety of a murder: they imply that it was necessary, justified, and for the social good. That there is an offender here, in the form of Temple, is a central question when one looks at the meaning of redemption; but from the legal viewpoint Nancy is the offender, and from the criminological perspective one must confront the question of whether we are going to condemn the offense as inherently evil. Berdyaev tells us that evil begets evil, crime begets crime, and that is why the murder of Lizaveta may be even more important than the slaying of her sister. Now, Temple's transgressions certainly led to others, by herself and by Nancy, but again, what of Nancy? What further evil was begot by the murder of the infant?

Nancy's position is an uncommon one, and the criminologist may put it aside as simply not sufficiently relevant to crime, as it is known in the modern world, to warrant that much attention. However, by extension, it is seen to have similarities with considerable crime, although it can hardly be said to be universal. In some respects, the murder of the child by Nancy may be closer to many crimes committed by individuals and by nation-states than are the murders of the two women by the Petersburg student. Nancy was no freedom fighter, hers were not politically motivated acts, they were not perpetrated in concert with others, but they do suggest a thread in common: the definition by the criminals of their own crimes as socially good and necessary. She was no political criminal, but philosophically Nancy has much in common with those who are. And they have grown in numbers, particularly with the strong movement among prisoners toward politicization of their "ordinary" crimes. They act in the name of freedom to which they have given their allegiance, and, like Nancy, for their goals they are willing to sacrifice their lives. They would never deny their culpability, any more than would Nancy, unless denial were for the purpose of freeing themselves not so as to enjoy life outside prison but so that they could repeatedly work in the same direction, including the commission of more and similar crimes.

In sum, Faulkner strongly suggests the very reverse of Dostoevsky: namely, that the crime was justified, so much so that its perpetrator could not conceptualize it as crime. Nancy is dying for the sins of another, it is true, but unlike Christ she has sinned, too—unless Faulkner would deny that hers was a sin, and this is dangerously close to the position to which he brings us. To the surrounding world, Nancy was a sinner, but the same could have been said of Christ, who sinned against the Sanhedrin by preaching doctrines declared to be heresy. When questioned, Christ freely admitted his unorthodoxy, even as Nancy freely admits her crime. Furthermore, in ancient Judaism there was no significant distinction between the moral and the legal orders, so that transgressions against one made the transgressor both sinner and criminal.

Like Christ, Nancy is to be crucified, but her rebirth will be in the next life, in contrast to Raskolnikov's in this one. If we equate Nancy with Christ, as Faulkner evidently intended, are we to conclude that her crime, unorthodox as it was, and a transgression against the legal order, was not evil—that it was both necessary and justified? What compounds the issue and confuses it is that Nancy makes the decision to be crucified herself: she assumes responsibility in the fullest existential sense. She was not driven, forced, or compelled by Temple, and refuses even to reveal the circumstances of the murder, a revelation that might save her life (if she did, the crucifixion would fail and with it her Christlike purity). One way out of this dilemma is to place responsibility for the murder of the infant on Temple; but although she instigated it, she did not commit it, and once one makes that shift the entire process whereby the performer must accept responsibility for his act is violated.

Alberto Moravia, in a commentary both on Dostoevsky and on the Soviet regime, finds in Raskolnikov's repudiation of his crime, and repudiation of his self-justification, an anti-Marxist statement that evil, in the form of murder and other crime, is never justified by one's belief in the goal that it is to save humanity:

> In short, for the Marxists evil does not really exist, since it is solely a matter of a social evil which can be eliminated by the revolution. But for Dostoevsky evil exists as an individual fact, in each man's heart, and expresses itself precisely in the violent means used by the revolution. With

their historic and social justifications the Marxists can wash clean even the blackest of consciences. Dostoevsky rejects this sort of cleansing and affirms the ineradicable existence of evil.[5]

Marxist critics can find a response to this: that there is evil that the revolution seeks to eradicate, and that Raskolnikov acted alone, not merely against the pawnbroker but against society; but a revolution, like a slave revolt, or terrorism against Nazis, for example, is collective. It is a civil war of one group against the evil other.

However, one turns to Faulkner and finds there an even stronger and more irreconcilable conflict with Dostoevsky. In Nancy, Faulkner has created the reverse of a Raskolnikov. In *Requiem for a Nun*, Faulkner has justified individual murder, and by implication any other criminal act, when the perpetrator believes, with considerable reason, that the motives are altruistic, that the act is performed as a social good. In the view of Marxists (or at least those who accept Dostoevsky, for he has undergone an ebb and flow of official acceptance by the regime since the revolution), Dostoevsky is not suggesting that all killing is wrong, but that no individual can be the god who is capable of making this decision for himself, and that to kill in order to prove that one is such a god only establishes the reverse.

There is nothing in Raskolnikov's story that demonstrates that all violence must be rejected (yet nothing that indicates that it may sometimes be justified: this is not a question which Dostoevsky addresses). Even Gandhi would use violence in defense of his home, his family, and possibly himself, and much as we might all be nostalgic for the days of internationalism and pacifism, and when nonviolence was a virtue in itself—days and years that may never have existed except in our hopes, fantasies, and chimeras—many would extend Gandhi's defense of his home to include the homeland. Here, there is almost certain indication that Gandhi would not have agreed, but when his disciples came to power, they did. One need not resort to von Clausewitz to know that defense is a peculiar and almost indefinable concept, and that some would include in the protection of their homes and homeland the effort, including the violence, to retake the home and homeland that they define as having been improperly, perhaps criminally, seized from them, or to make "preventive strikes" so as to defend themselves from expected or allegedly planned attack.

The problem posed and studied by Dostoevsky is answered only for such events as are symbolized by Raskolnikov's evil deed, but no more, and it is reopened by Faulkner. It is relevant for at least a portion of modern-day criminality, including political terrorism, wars of states against dissidents and of dissidents against states, and politically motivated individual and group violence. Neither Raskolnikov nor Nancy gives us an answer, nor is it to be found in the characters in *Lord Jim* and *Crime and Punishment* who choose the route of suicide (Brierly and Svidrigaylov, respectively), nor in Temple, whose weak confession is meant only to wipe clean her own slate. It is the question of crime for a higher purpose, not merely civil disobedience and lawbreaking of the type committed by Martin Luther King, but which could result in injury to no one except the perpetrators of the disobedience, who could be and were in fact beaten and jailed.[6] Political leaders, rebels, moral philosophers will struggle with this issue, as will criminologists, and if they cannot find answers they can at least obtain insights into the minds of the perpetrators in Dostoevsky and Faulkner, and many who preceded and followed them.

In a social world—and this is true, but less so, of the physical world as well—in which one always encounters gradations and continua, but seldom quanta and discontinuities, it may be useful to divide crime into two realms: acts committed for higher reasons, often at the sacrifice of the life or freedom of the offender, and those perpetrated to gratify greed or passion. Some will look to Dostoevsky and, like Moravia, reject this division because they are weary of violence and hope only for a world at peace. But the two types of acts will not dissolve into one because we wish it so, and if the crimes of greed and passion are more numerous, the selfless ones may have greater implications for influencing, even molding, the lives of all of us. In Faulkner, this takes the form of an altruistic self-sacrifice by one individual, but the acceptance or rejection of Faulkner's vision has meaning for the political scene and for political crime. Criminologists will continue to study crime that is justified in the eyes of its perpetrator: the nature of the events, the types of persons involved in them, their backgrounds and beliefs, their adamant determination, how the events are planned in conspiracy, sometimes set off by mass media, or catalyzed by what they define as provocation, and how they are fostered or diminished by repression or concession. But as for going into the minds of persons committing such offenses, if they are to be called offenses, social scientists could do worse than to look at the portraits by men and women of letters; in fact, it is difficult to imagine how they could do better.

Yet, somehow, I am reluctant to leave this theme without the admission that for the ordinary crime—whatever that may be—and for the ordinary criminal—an elusive abstraction—the literary images may not be extremely illuminating. They might even be misleading. It is true that other examples might have been chosen, but few come to mind that would have told us about people who are not consumed by their own feelings of guilt, who are most successful (in their relationships both with self and society) in evading responsibility for their acts, and who do not walk into the police station to surrender when there is a paucity of evidence against them. The literary artists have thrown light on salvation through pollution, salvation through the gutters (expressions for which I am indebted to Shlomo Shoham), rebirth through suffering, atonement, and sacrifice, but they have given little illumination into the minds of those who revel in the joys and pleasures of life "earned" by inflicting sufferings on others.[7] Only Temple Drake and Moll Flanders escape without penalty—even Jean Valjean suffers, but this is for what might be termed society's crime, not his. Temple does feel guilt and does endure punishment, though the evil is neither recognized nor expiated and she is incapable of absolution. We are left with Moll Flanders, who cannot know the meaning of repentance: she repents only for the occasions when she was apprehended, but even this is turned into good fortune for her.

Are the literary masters, then, alienated from the mass of criminal events, and in turning attention to individuals, have they created and chosen those situations and persons in which universality is lacking? Must one conclude that in literature and criminology we not only have two cultures with different methods and goals, but that they have examined two dissimilar aspects of the same phenomenon, and that in literature one finds the less typical and therefore the less significant of the two for an understanding of criminal minds and criminal events? I do not quite think so. What literature has portrayed, from the Greek tragedians to the present, and exemplified by Raskolnikov particularly, is the capacity of humanity for transgression: in Dostoevsky this is especially illuminated by the goodness of the man who carries out the two murders. Here Dostoevsky provides an important insight into the workings of the mind and consciousness. The latter cannot be limited to something as specific as motive. The consciousness of Raskolnikov is ever obliging in generating a sufficiency of reasons for his acts. We watch him lost in a maze of motivations, never quite certain what it is that is inducing him to commit murder, or, after the event, just what had been his own motivations. He continually spies on himself in an effort to penetrate his own psychology and attain the self-knowledge that he needs if he is to assume responsibility for his hideous acts, or if he is to be successful in rationalizing them away so that he believes himself free of responsibility. And this idea of the criminal in search of his own motive, so new and original in the character created by Dostoevsky, was later to be refined by Kafka. For in Joseph K. we have the enlightened but estranged individual who not only lacks a clear understanding of his motives but is also ignorant of the nature of his wrongdoing, although he is ready to accept responsibility and guilt.

In Lord Jim, Conrad has portrayed mankind's abilities to find end-less mechanisms to avoid responsibility for conduct, and at the same time the realization of the need to accept that responsibility in order for rebirth to be possible. In Sophocles, the responsibility is taken by Oedi-pus even though it was his destiny to commit parricide and incest, and he neither knew his relationship to his father and mother nor had criminal intent.

Evil begets evil: the unplanned murder as a result of the planned murder, the terrible fate of Ethan Frome resulting from the expected abandonment of his wife through suicide, the murder of the child by Nancy as a result of the numerous transgressions of Temple. Finally, there is the potential of all humans to be redeemed, to cleanse them-selves, to reach a state of absolution, through suffering and expiation. These are all capacities, and are not invariably fulfilled.

What, then, does the novel offer to our understanding of the social realities of crime and punishment? How does it enrich our comprehen-sion of these and related phenomena? We return to the questions posed in the introductory chapter.

From a structural point of view, the narrative dimensions of the novels under consideration reduce reality to specific points in time and abstract from the multitude of experiences certain sets of actions and states of being, logically linked together in a causal chain or sequence of events that are intelligible in themselves and illuminating of other simi-lar though not identical experiences. In other words, the novel is a deliberate construction of a world in order to make clear certain ideas implicit in the imagined people and their actions. The fictive world does not sprawl before us as the real one does, distracting us from a main line of activities. The social worlds of fiction are stories with themes, with beginnings and ends, not fragmented arguments elaborated with tables, but flesh and blood embodiments of significant social facts. But if the implicit conclusions do not coincide with the elaborate statistics, seemingly lifeless but actually written in blood, then the incongruities must be faced, and one or another of the approaches discarded.

Being purged of the accidents and uncertainties of existence, the seven works in these essays have the stabilities of an algebra containing organized ideas, events, and persons, so that the reality they describe is not mysterious or absurd, but clear, simple, and, in varying degrees, familiar. Of course, a novel can be deaf to the world which gives it life and fail to convey the ethos and pith of its culture. Or it may mold a social world that is a mirror image of reality, but nonetheless devoid of life.

With these cautions in mind, a reader may find the novel a major source of knowledge. It need not be viewed as escapist, utopian, illusionary, or entertaining, but as a lucid art form that imparts information by reproducing as only it can the particulars of social differences and similarities. Its burden is to give an immediate account of the situation of people, their origins, classes, histories, and predicaments, and insofar as it does this, it teaches, informs, and expands the horizons of our knowledge.

The themes of the novelists speak to criminology, they are relevant and contemporary. When their insights are wedded to the findings of social science, using rigorous approaches and scientifically developed methods, there will be illumination on the dark side of human activity. Sociologists, psychologists, and other behavioral scientists, those who specialize in the study of crime and deviance particularly, can follow in the footsteps of Freud and walk humbly in this valley of light.

NOTES

1. This is part of the general literature known as victimology. The first major work on this theme was Hans von Hentig, *The Criminal and His Victim* (New Haven: Yale University Press, 1946; reprinted with preface by Marvin Wolfgang, New York: Schocken Books, 1979). Victim precipitation in murder cases is described by Marvin Wolfgang in *Patterns in Criminal Homicide* (Philadelphia: University of Pennsylvania Press, 1958), in forcible rape by Menachem Amir in *Patterns in Forcible Rape* (Chicago: University of Chicago Press, 1971).

2. Vyacheslav Ivanov, "The Revolt Against Mother Earth," from *Freedom and the Tragic Life* (New York: Noonday, 1952), reprinted in Feodor Dostoevsky, *Crime and Punishment*, ed. George Gibian and trans. Jessie Coulson, Norton Critical Edition (New York: Norton, 1975), pp. 577–585.

3. This is reminiscent of a story of a policeman accused of killing a young man in his custody. The policeman was exonerated and a social scientist, describing the event, wrote that "the trigger moved," as if the policeman had had nothing to do with that movement.

4. Gilbert Geis, "Jeremy Bentham," in Hermann Mannheim, ed., *Pioneers in Criminology*, 2nd ed. (Montclair, N.J.: Patterson Smith, 1972), p. 60.

5. Alberto Moravia, "The Marx-Dostoevsky Duel," in Dostoevsky, *Crime and Punishment*, p. 644; originally published in *Encounter*, November 1956, pp. 3–5.

6. There could be injury to the opponents of King, but those injured would have to assume responsibility for their own actions and the consequences thereof.

7. Shlomo Shoham has written extensively on this theme. See S. Giora Shoham, *The Myth of Tantalus: A Scaffolding for an Ontological Personality Theory* (St. Lucia, Queensland: University of Queensland Press, 1979), *Salvation Through the Gutters: Deviance and Transcendence* (Washington, D.C.: Hemisphere, 1979), and *Social Deviance* (New York: Gardner, 1976).

Bibliographical and Critical Literature on the Seven Novels

Feodor Dostoevsky: *Crime and Punishment*

Feodor Dostoevsky (1821–1881) is a towering figure in Russian literature. *Crime and Punishment* appeared in a magazine, *Russki Vestnik*, in 1866, and was then published in book form in St. Petersburg in a somewhat shorter version that became the established text. It was introduced to the English-speaking world by Constance Garnett, who devoted her life to translating an entire body of major nineteenth-century Russian literature. Although her translations are still in print, and the debt owed to her is almost unequalled in the history of the rendition of literature from one language to another, her work has for the most part been superseded by translations that are more accurate, are of superior literary style, and do not reflect the professed moral codes of Victorian and Edwardian England.

The literature on both the author and the novel is vast. *The Notebooks for Crime and Punishment,* ed. and trans. by Edward Wasiolek (Chicago: University of Chicago Press, 1967), is based upon a publication that appeared in Moscow and Leningrad in 1931. Wasiolek is also the author of *Dostoevsky: The Major Fiction* (Cambridge, Mass.: MIT Press, 1964). André Gide wrote an influential work entitled *Dostoevsky* (New York: New Directions, 1961; originally published in English in 1925). There is an essay on *Crime and Punishment* in Edwin M. Moseley, *Pseudonyms of Christ in the Mod-*

ern Novel: Motifs and Methods (Pittsburgh: University of Pittsburgh Press, 1962). Among other works of interest are Helen Muchnic, *Russian Writers: Notes and Essays* (New York: Random House, 1965); Vyacheslav Ivanov, *Freedom and the Tragic Life: A Study in Dostoevsky* (New York: Noonday, 1952); and Temira Pachmuss, *F. M. Dostoevsky: Dualism and Synthesis of the Human Soul* (Carbondale: Southern Illinois University Press, 1963). Robert Louis Jackson has edited *Twentieth Century Interpretations of Crime and Punishment: A Collection of Critical Essays* (Englewood Cliffs, N.J.: Prentice-Hall, 1973), an outstanding volume of essays and interpretations of *Crime and Punishment*. A collection of important essays is found in the latter part of the Norton edition (cited below), and contains works by Ortega y Gasset, Philip Rahv, Nicholas Berdyaev, Karen Horney, and R. D. Laing, among others.

The Garnett translation remains in print, in Dutton, Modern Library, and other editions. A translation by Jessie Coulson, published by Oxford University Press in 1953, is used in the Norton Critical Edition, ed. by George Gibian (New York: Norton, 1975). A translation by Sidney Monas is available from New American Library, and one by David Magarshack from Penguin. Laurel has published the Garnett translation in two editions, one an abridgment by Edmund Fuller which is not recommended.

Daniel Defoe: *Moll Flanders*

Daniel Defoe (ca. 1661–1731) was one of the major English writers of his times. *Moll Flanders* was published in London in 1721 or 1722 (the exact year is uncertain) and went through many editions and changes of title until it came to be known simply by the name of its central character.

Ian Watt deals with *Moll Flanders* in his influential work *The Rise of the Novel* (Berkeley: University of California Press, 1957). Leslie Stephen wrote a major essay in his *English Literature and Society in the Eighteenth Century* (New York: Barnes & Noble, 1955, based on lectures delivered in 1903 and first published in 1904). Mark Schorer wrote the introduction to the Modern Library edition, and *Moll Flanders* is one of the important works that he discusses in *The World We Imagine* (New York: Farrar, Straus & Giroux, 1968). Among other critical works dealing with the author and novel, see Everett Zimmerman, *Defoe and the Novel* (Berkeley: University of California Press, 1975) and James Sutherland, *Daniel Defoe: A Critical Study* (Cambridge, Mass.: Harvard University Press, 1971). Essays on Defoe and

Conrad are found in Edward Wagenknecht, *Cavalcade of the English Novel* (New York: Henry Holt, 1954) and Elizabeth Drew, *The Novel: A Modern Guide to Fifteen English Masterpieces* (New York: Norton, 1963).

In addition to the Modern Library edition, the book is in print by New American Library, Penguin, Airmont, Houghton Mifflin, Washington Square Press, and other imprints.

Victor Hugo: *Les Misérables*

Victor Hugo (1802–1885) was a prolific French novelist, dramatist, and poet. *Les Misérables* was published in Paris and Brussels in 1862, was an immediate success, and went into many editions, including abridgments and single episodes published as separate books, with the consent of the author. In 1927, an early version of the novel, *Les Misères,* was published in Paris.

Translations of *Les Misérables* are known to exist in dozens of languages, including Esperanto. Two different English translations appeared in 1862, and these were followed by several others. An 1895 abridgment was described on the title page, "The whole story intact; episodes and detailed descriptions only omitted." A similar abridgment, published by the Literary Guild in 1954, had the following statement: "The editors have deleted large blocks of unnecessary narration, description, and unimportant historical data."

The critical literature on Hugo and interpretations of *Les Misérables* are almost entirely in French. The best guide to this literature is Elliott M. Grant, *Victor Hugo: Select and Critical Bibliography* (Chapel Hill: University of North Carolina Press, 1967), which has excellent references with annotations. Grant calls attention to P. Abraham et al., "Articles Commemorating the Centenary of *Les Misérables,*" which appeared in *Euro* 40 (February/March 1962): 3–209.

An early enthusiastic supporter of Hugo was the English lyric poet Algernon Charles Swinburne, author of *A Study of Victor Hugo* (London: Chatto & Windus, 1886, repr. Folcroft Library Editions, 1976). Lytton Strachey wrote on Hugo in *Landmarks in French Literature* (New York: Oxford University Press, 1969; first published in 1912). Commentary on Hugo, with special reference to *Les Misérables,* is found in Horatio Smith, *Makers of French Literature* (Freeport, L.I.: Books for Libraries Press, 1969; first published in 1937) and David Owen Evans, *Social Romanticism in Frame* (Oxford: At the Clarendon Press, 1951). A French volume appeared in 1970 entitled *Victor Hugo*

Publie Les Misérables (Correspondance avec Albert Lacroix, août 1861–juillet 1862). Lacroix was the Belgian publisher of the 1862 edition.

There are many editions and translations, in cloth and paper, in English and in French, currently available in the United States. Dodd, Mead has an abridged edition which is recommended.

Joseph Conrad: *Lord Jim*

Joseph Conrad (1857–1924) was born in the Ukraine, son of Polish parents, christened Jósef Teodor Konrad Nalecz Korzenioski (some versions reverse the first two names). His mother tongue was Polish, but after he became fluent in French and English he adopted the latter as the language for his writing career.

Lord Jim was first published in *Blackwood's Magazine* in 1899, and made its appearance in book form in both England and the United States the following year. There is a large volume of critical literature on Conrad and specifically on this novel. Some of the highlights are given here: Albert Guerard, *Conrad the Novelist* (Cambridge, Mass.: Harvard University Press, 1958; repr. New York: Atheneum, 1967); Peter J. Glassman, *Language and Being: Joseph Conrad and the Literature of Personality* (New York: Columbia University Press, 1976); Edward W. Said, *Joseph Conrad and the Fiction of Autobiography* (Cambridge, Mass.: Harvard University Press, 1966); John Gordan, *Joseph Conrad: The Making of a Novelist* (New York: Russell & Russell, 1940; repr. 1963); Arthur Mizener, *The Sense of Life in the Modern Novel* (Boston: Houghton Mifflin, 1964); C. B. Cox, *Joseph Conrad: The Modern Imagination* (Totowa, N.J.: Rowman & Littlefield, 1974); and Ian Watt, *Conrad in the Nineteenth Century* (Berkeley: University of California Press, 1980).

The narrator in *Lord Jim,* Marlow, is the subject of an essay by W. Y. Tindall in Robert C. Rathburn and Martin Steinman, eds., *From Jane Austen to Joseph Conrad* (Minneapolis: University of Minnesota Press, 1958). Material on Conrad is found in Frank R. Leavis, *The Great Tradition* (New York: New York University Press, 1964), and in Dorothy Van Ghent, *The English Novel: Form and Function* (New York: Rinehart, 1963).

There are several collections of essays on both the author and the novel. Norman Sherry is editor of *Conrad: The Critical Heritage* (Boston: Routledge, 1973). Marvin Mudrick edited *Conrad: A Collection of Critical Essays* (Englewood Cliffs, N.J.: Prentice-Hall, 1966). Robert S.

Kuehn brought together *Twentieth Century Interpretations of Lord Jim: A Collection of Critical Essays* (Englewood Cliffs, N.J.: Prentice-Hall, 1969).

Thomas Moser edited the Norton Critical Edition of *Lord Jim*, which contains about one hundred pages of some of the most important criticism of the work and a bibliography of writings on both the author and the novel. In addition to the Norton edition, *Lord Jim* is available from Penguin, Doubleday, Houghton Mifflin, Dutton, New American Library, and many others. Laurel has an excellent edition, with an introduction by Albert Guerard.

Edith Wharton: *Ethan Frome*

Edith Wharton (1862–1937) was an American novelist who spent a large part of her adult life in Europe. *Ethan Frome* was published by Scribner in 1911. An early draft of the novel was written in French and published in July 1952 in *Yale University Library Gazette*.

Among the writings on Wharton are Blake Nevins, *Edith Wharton: A Study of Her Fiction* (Berkeley: University of California Press, 1961); and Marilyn Jones Lyde, *Edith Wharton: Convention and Morality in the Work of a Novelist* (Norman: University of Oklahoma Press, 1959). Irving Howe edited *Edith Wharton: A Collection of Critical Essays* (Englewood Cliffs, N.J.: Prentice-Hall, 1965), which contains writings by Louis Auchincloss, Edmund Wilson, Alfred Kazin, and others; the only material specifically related to *Ethan Frome* is a brief excerpt from the book by Nevins, mentioned above. A biography with psychoanalytic interpretations of the writings (including *Ethan Frome*) was written by Cynthia Griffin Wolff, *A Feast of Words: The Triumph of Edith Wharton* (New York: Oxford University Press, 1977). A chapter on *Ethan Frome* appears in Richard H. Lawson, *Edith Wharton* (New York: Ungar, 1977); and one by Lionel Trilling, entitled "The Morality of Inertia," is found in his book *A Gathering of Fugitives* (New York: Harcourt Brace Jovanovich, 1978; first published in 1956).

In 1935 the novel was dramatized by Owen and Donald Davis, and played in New York and elsewhere. It was a theatrical success, starring Ruth Gordon as Mattie, Pauline Lord as Zeena, and Raymond Massie as Ethan. The drama was published by Scribner the following year.

In addition to its regular edition, Scribner has issued the novel in a form edited by Blake Nevins, *Edith Wharton's Ethan Frome: The Story with Sources and Commentary* (1968). There are several critical essays in the appendix, including the one by Lionel Trilling that is mentioned above.

William Faulkner: *Sanctuary* and *Requiem for a Nun*

William Faulkner (1897–1962), American writer, won the Nobel Prize for Literature in 1949. *Sanctuary* was published in 1931, and *Requiem for a Nun* appeared just twenty years later. Despite the difficulty of his language, Faulkner has been widely translated.

The critical literature on Faulkner may already exceed that of any other American writer of this century in size and scope. In addition to numerous books and articles, there are dictionaries, guides to his characters, indexes, bibliographies, glossaries, anthologies. A few major works are cited here: Richard P. Adams, *Faulkner: Myth and Motion* (Princeton, N.J.: Princeton University Press, 1968); Melvin Beckman, *Faulkner: The Major Years—A Critical Study* (Bloomington: Indiana University Press, 1966); Irving Howe, *William Faulkner: A Critical Study* (New York: Random House, 1952); and George C. Bedell, *Kierkegaard and Faulkner: Modalities of Existence* (Baton Rouge: Louisiana State University Press, 1973). A work in French is of special interest: Jean Weisberger, *Faulkner et Dostoïevski: Confluences et Influences* (Paris et Bruxelles: Presses Universitaires, 1968). Students of *Sanctuary* might wish to look at Gerald Langford, *Faulkner's Revision of "Sanctuary": A Collation of the Unrevised Galleys and the Published Book* (Austin: University of Texas Press, 1972).

There are several collections of Faulkner criticism. One is Frederick J. Hoffman and Olga W. Vickery, *William Faulkner: Three Decades of Criticism* (New York: Harcourt Brace Jovanovich, rev. ed., 1960), which contains important essays by Conrad Aiken, Jean-Paul Sartre, Alfred Kazin, Robert Penn Warren, and others (there are no essays specifically on either *Sanctuary* or *Requiem*, but the bibliographies include twenty-four citations on the former, twelve on the latter). Two essays on *Sanctuary* are found in an excellent collection edited by Robert Penn Warren, *Faulkner: A Collection of Critical Essays* (Englewood Cliffs, N.J.: Prentice-Hall, 1966).

For an interpretation of Temple Drake's testimony against Lee Goodwin, see Peter Lisca, "Some New Light on Faulkner's *Sanctuary*," in *Faulkner Studies* 2 (Spring 1953): 5–9. In two books devoted to the women in Faulkner, there are chapters on Temple Drake; these are Sally R. Page, *Faulkner's Women: Characterization and Meaning* (Deland, Fla.: Everett/Edwards, 1972) and David Williams, *Faulkner's Women: The Myth and the Muse* (Montreal: McGill University Press, 1977). Temple is also discussed at some length by Leslie Fiedler in *Love and Death in the American Novel* (New York: Dell, 1960), and the rape is discussed by W. M. Frohock in *The Novel of Violence in America*

(Boston: Beacon Press, 1964; first published in 1950). An early essay on the rape by Wyndham Lewis, "Moralist with a Corncob," first appeared in 1934 and is found in that author's *Men Without Art* (New York: Russell and Russell, 1964).

Sanctuary and *Requiem for a Nun* are available in Vintage paper editions. In the past, they have been published together in one volume.

Selected List of Literature for Further Study

From the abundant literature that presents images of crime, punishment, redemption, and atonement, I suggest below a few items for reading and analysis:

Anderson, Sherwood. *Beyond Desire*
Baldwin, James. *Giovanni's Room*
Camus, Albert. *The Stranger*
Coleridge, Samuel. "The Rime of the Ancient Mariner"
Crane, Stephen. *Maggie: A Girl of the Streets*
Dante Alighieri. *The Inferno*
Dreiser, Theodore. *Sister Carrie*
      An American Tragedy
Eliot, George. *Adam Bede*
Faulkner, William. *The Sound and the Fury*
      Light in August
      Intruder in the Dust
      Absalom, Absalom!
Flaubert, Gustave. *Madame Bovary*
Genet, Jean. *Our Lady of the Flowers*
Gide, André. *The Immoralist*
Goethe, Johann Wolfgang von. *Faust*
Green, Julien. *Moira*
Hardy, Thomas. *Tess of the d'Urbervilles*
      The Mayor of Casterbridge

Hawthorne, Nathaniel. *The Scarlet Letter*
Jackson, Shirley. "The Lottery"
Kafka, Franz. *The Trial*
            "In the Penal Colony"
Lee, Harper. *To Kill a Mockingbird*
Mann, Thomas. *Death in Venice*
            The Holy Sinner
Marlowe, Christopher. *Edward II*
            Doctor Faustus
Milton, John. *Paradise Lost*
            Paradise Regained
O'Flaherty, Liam. *The Informer*
O'Neill, Eugene. *Mourning Becomes Electra*
            The Iceman Cometh
            Long Day's Journey into Night
Sartre, Jean-Paul. *No Exit*
            Dirty Hands
            "The Wall"
Shakespeare, William. "The Rape of Lucrece"
            Hamlet
            Macbeth
            King Lear
            Julius Caesar
            Othello
Solzhenitsyn, Alexander. *Cancer Ward*
Sophocles. *Oedipus Rex*
Steinbeck, John. *The Pearl*
Stendhal. *The Red and the Black*
Styron, William. *Lie Down in Darkness*
            Sophie's Choice
Tolstoi, Leo. *Resurrection*
Werfel, Franz. "Not the Murderer"
Wilde, Oscar. "The Ballad of Reading Gaol"
Wright, Richard. *Native Son*

Almost all of Shakespeare's tragedies, and many of his histories and romances, could be added to the list of five plays mentioned above. To *Oedipus Rex,* one might add the two other dramas making up the Oedipus trilogy, and the list could be extended to include the complete extant Greek tragedies (that is, the complete works of Sophocles, Euripides, and Aeschylus).

Of the four short stories in the above list, those by Jackson, Kafka, and Sartre are found in many anthologies and in works by the three authors. "Not the Murderer" is a translation of *Nicht der Mörder, der Ermordete ist Schuldig,* a story that had a strong influence in the early years of victimology. The translation is found in Werfel's *Twilight of a World.*

A survey of American literature written by convicts and exconvicts, much of it dealing with crime and prison, is found in H. Bruce Franklin, *The Victim as Criminal and Artist: Literature from the American Prison* (New York: Oxford University Press, 1978). Many avenues for further study are indicated in the works discussed by Franklin.

Index